Getting ready for
marriage

Getting ready for marriage

David R. Mace

OLIPHANTS

OLIPHANTS
MARSHALL, MORGAN & SCOTT
116 Baker Street
London W1M 2BB

Copyright © 1972 by Abingdon Press
First published in Great Britain 1974
ISBN 0 551 00534 3

Printed in Great Britain by
Hunt Barnard Printing Ltd., Aylesbury, Bucks.

Dedicated, with affection and gratitude,

to Gladys
My one and only sister
and the best in the world

I did not want one word of advice about Everett, myself, or the married state. I awaited marriage as revelation. I no more wanted a premarriage résumé of what lay ahead than I want an inventory of Christmas presents before Christmas. I intended to launch into the state of Holy Matrimony un-nourished by so much as a crumb of worldy knowledge; and I did so launch. The trouble was, Everett was launched in exactly the same manner. And what we were headed for was not so much a collision course as a complete miss.

JESSAMYN WEST, A Matter of Time.

Preface

This is an unusual book, and this is my opportunity to explain what I had in mind in the writing of it. I have spent a good part of my life in counselling people about marriage, and have found it to be a rewarding experience. In some cases, however, it was too late to repair the damage already done. In others, it became clear that the couple had never possessed the resources needed to give to each other the happiness they expected, and indeed demanded. Becoming aware of these painful facts has, I think, in most instances helped husband and wife to make the best of their situation, or to go their separate ways without adding to their personal tragedy the additional hurt of needless recrimination.

However, as the marriage counsellor reflects on his work and reviews in his mind the long procession of men and women in whose pain and perplexity he has been deeply involved, he is at times overwhelmed as he realizes the absurdity of our whole policy, or lack of policy, regarding marriage, the nuclear relationship upon which the human community is built.

We allow people to drift into this relationship, with all its maddening complexity, on pink clouds of romantic sentiment. We send them forth, after solemn ceremonies involving the blessing of religion and the hearty goodwill of relatives and friends, on a joint enterprise concerning which we have made no serious endeavour to enlighten them; and in which, as the dreary statistics make plain, a substantial number of them are doomed to fail.

We are prepared to spend considerable effort and money on the wedding, which is over in a few hours; yet we complacently leave to chance the outcome of the marriage, which is expected to last a lifetime. This has always seemed to me to be one of the most dramatic manifestations of the fact that, for all our proud boasts that we live in an era of rationality, we do nothing of the sort.

We marriage counsellors have tried to do something about this. We have developed the concept of marriage preparation. Drawing on our knowledge of the factors that cause marriages to fail, and tracing those factors back to their origins, we have discovered that many of them could have been eliminated if the couple had been helped, early in their association, to recognize the dangers and take appropriate steps to avoid them. If we are able by careful planning to anticipate and eliminate the awesome hazards involved in a voyage to the moon, it should not be beyond our power to steer most people around the hazards of matrimony. So we have reasoned, and offered our services.

These services, alas, have been largely spurned. The community is preoccupied with the plight of married couples already in serious trouble; and we have had to expend most of our efforts in the costly attempt to help them, despite the fact that the next group of marital breakdowns is already in process of being prepared for subsequent disaster and that preventing such future disaster would yield immensely greater rewards for a similar output of effort. Every well-qualified marriage counsellor would rather spend his time with couples thinking about marriage, for whom he can often do a great deal, than with the desperate victims of marital shipwreck whose shrill cries for help assail his ears. But it is these latter who continually demand his services and consume his time, while the others go unheeding on their way to seek him out decades later when they in turn have made havoc of their marriages.

I have written this book is order to raise my voice in a plea that we should end this foolishness. My purpose is not, however, simply to cry in protest. What I prefer to do is to offer a plan, a proposal, that may provide something better. Let me outline this plan.

Professional people who undertake marriage preparation develop their own individual patterns. But the most experienced of them, I find, have reached a high degree of consensus about the most effective ways of helping a couple get ready for marriage.

Most of us began with the 'facts-of-life' approach – offering knowledge about the various aspects of married life, on the assumption that ignorance was the prime cause of marital trouble and that individualized education was the couple's greatest need. There was much truth in this assertion a few decades ago, and there is still validity in this approach. But this is emphatically not the primary task of marriage preparation, and if this is all that is offered its impact is likely to be superficial. There are good reasons for saying this which need not be elaborated here.

The second approach is to encourage and help the couple to make a careful evaluation of themselves, of each other, and of their relationship. This is far more effective than feeding them general facts about married life. This process dissolves the pink clouds and brings the perception of the couple down to the level of reality, which is emphatically where they are going to have to live when they become man and wife. Moreover, it deals with them where they are, now, because it rests on the assumption that *the best way to enable a couple to move toward a successful relationship in the future is to help them to achieve a successful relationship here and now.*

The third approach is strictly speaking not an approach at all but a response. It involves counselling with the couple concerning specific difficulties in their relationship about which they have asked for help. This and this alone should be called 'pre-marital counselling', although in practice we confuse the issue by applying this term to the whole preparation process, which may often involve no counselling in the technical sense at all.

The core of marriage preparation, therefore, lies in the second approach, with some of the first included incidentally, and the possibility that the third will develop as a result of the new awareness that the couple will be almost sure to achieve. Ideally, all this should take place in a series of interviews between the couple and an experienced person who is qualified to provide knowledge, to foster self-awareness, and to undertake counselling as it is required. I firmly and unhesitatingly affirm this to be the best way.

However, the situation we face is that large numbers of people, and their parents, have only the dimmest comprehension of all this, and therefore they are quite poorly motivated to seek the service that could make a significant difference to their chances of marital success. My plan is to meet this difficulty by putting as much as possible of the marriage preparation process into the form of a book and urging parents and friends to put it in the hands of couples as a token of goodwill. Once this is done, my hope is, naturally, that the couple will then read the book.

What I have done in these pages is to offer my readers, as far as is possible, exactly the programme of marriage preparation which I would go through with them if they came to see me professionally. They can thus, from a safe distance, involve themselves in the process of looking at themselves and at each other that I would try to facilitate if I were working with them directly. If they undertake at all seriously the simple assignments I have set them, they will soon be seeing their relationship more realistically and communicating with each other at a deeper level.

Some need no more than this. If they encounter no serious problems as they do their 'homework' together, they will have the satisfaction of knowing that they have met the tests and are ready for marriage. They will be in the position of couples whom the counsellor dismisses with his blessing, because he has every confidence that they are facing their future marriage realistically and have both the will and the wit to succeed in it.

Others who take the assignments seriously will, no doubt, find the going harder. They may manage to work through their immediate conflicts, using the procedures I have explained to them, without the need for further assistance; and if they do this it will greatly reinforce their confidence that they will likewise be able to face future conflicts when, as is likely, they arise. If they find themselves poorly informed about particular aspects of marriage, I have provided them with a selected list of books and some information about what they contain.

We are left with those who need face-to-face counselling about problems which they simply will not be able to resolve by themselves. No book can do for them what is necessary, yet a book may bring home to them the fact that they must seek counselling help, and that it makes sense to do so. At that point, I have constituted myself a referral service. At various points within the book, I have indicated to couples who, in terms of their own resources, find themselves at the end of the road, that the time has now come to get direct help from a professional person. And in an appendix I have tried, carefully and in detail, to guide them in the task of finding a counsellor who can give them the service they need. My hope is that, through reading the book and coming to understand how one marriage counsellor works, they may feel comfortable enough about the process to overcome their natural hesitation and make that vital appointment which may mark a turning point in their lives.

I hope I have made my purpose entirely clear. This is not just a book about marriage or even about marriage preparation. It is an attempt to reach couples directly and through the enlightened co-operation of parents and friends who wish them well, and to present to them earnestly the case for adequate marriage preparation. It is also an attempt actually to involve them in the process of marriage preparation as far as this can possibly be done through the written word, and to show those for whom this means is not adequate how they can find their way to the most competent help available to them.

'Books,' it has been said, 'are men's hearts in other men's hands.' My hope is that I have been able to convey in the pages of this book my heartfelt wish for the young couples who read it: that they may find through it the means to achieve in their marriages in the years ahead all the happiness and fulfillment which I have found in mine. I know of nothing better in human life that I could wish for them.

DAVID R. MACE

Contents

I Preparation
why it is so important

1 The Purpose of This Book

If you were planning a trip to Africa and consulted me about it because I happen to know Africa, I would be letting you down if I didn't tell you anything about the hazards and the discomforts you would encounter. Just because there are hazards, however, I wouldn't advise you not to go to Africa. I would make my knowledge available to you by telling you how to avoid the hazards. I would try to plan with you a pleasant, rewarding, trouble-free trip.

That is exactly what I want to do in helping you to prepare for your marriage. I have now been a marriage counsellor for some thirty-five years. I helped to get marriage counselling started in England and in several other parts of the world and played a part in developing it in the United States. During those years I have sat down for long hours with many couples in distress. I therefore know the hazards well, and there are plenty of them. But I am not discouraged about marriage on that account. On the contrary, I believe in it as much as, if not more than, I ever did. At its best it is a magnificent institution offering people tremendous rewards. Despite the difficulties, we know that married people in general are happier than single people, that they live longer, and that they enjoy better physical and mental health. These are facts, and I can add to them the testimony of my own personal experience. The best thing I ever did in my life was to get married. Marriage has brought me more happiness than all the other pleasant experiences of my life combined.

Why then do so many people run into trouble? There are many reasons, and I will try to give you some of them later. But I will give you the main reason now. It is because people don't get the help they need about marriage either before they begin or after they get married. My experience as a counsellor has brought me in touch with a great many married couples in trouble, and as I think of them two feelings sweep over me – compassion and anger. I feel compassion because these people, nearly all of them, wanted very much to achieve a warm, loving, mutually satisfying relationship. Yet they couldn't find what they sought, because they didn't understand the complexity of the task. They were ignorant, confused, bewildered. And when I think of their ignorance, then I begin to feel anger – anger with the smug, complacent indifference that prevents us from providing real help and guidance to most married people and to those moving into marriage. If all my long years as a marriage counsellor have taught me anything, it is that the unhappy marriages in our midst represent a tragic and inexcusable waste of the best human resources we have – the capacity for love and trust and tenderness and comradeship and mutual support that most men and women have within them and that they deeply desire to develop in marriage for their happiness and fulfilment.

Albert Einstein is reported to have said that the average person, as he goes through life, uses only about ten per cent of his mental powers. The remaining ninety per cent is wasted because it is never developed. Something like that, I believe, happens also in marriage. Large numbers of people have dreamed their dreams about the deep happiness a man and woman can find in each other and can shape into the rich experience of a shared life. But the fulfilment of the dream has eluded them, and as they have gone through life they have become bitter, restless, and dissatisfied. They had the potential to realize a shared life of lasting love, but they never managed to realize it.

In today's world there is plenty of cynicism about marriage. This of course is nothing new. Marriage has always been a favourite theme for the jokes of the entertainers. Cynicism has at its root a pang of wistfulness, and a cynic's destructiveness springs from his own concealed hurt. He is a disappointed, disillusioned person who has found life sour.

For that reason, the cynic is not a reliable guide to the state of marriage in our world today. Marriage has not been exposed as a fraud. It is not in a state of decline. Here is what Dr Paul Glick, one of the foremost American authorities on the subject, says of it, 'The more I study the subject, the more apparent it becomes; marriage is regarded as the happiest, healthiest and most desired state of human existence. We get divorced not because we don't like marriage, but to find a better marriage partner. We live longer and are healthier if we are married. Marriage is the central fact of our lives.'* Marriage, in short, is still viewed as a happy, rewarding experience to which most people earnestly aspire. It is a misfortune that many fail to realize this hope. I believe however that it is a misfortune that can be remedied. Many, many more people could enjoy the blessing of a truly happy marriage, if only. . . .

If only. . . . What we need to do is to see marriage as a task, as a goal that is certainly difficult to attain but not unattainable. If we drift into marriage, thinking of it as a free gift handed to us on a silver platter by a smiling providence and guaranteed of itself to bring us lasting bliss, we are being utterly unrealistic. 'We are in love, and that will solve all problems' is a very dangerous philosophy for any couple. Marriage is demanding. It calls for intelligence and effort and maturity and patience to achieve the rewards it has to offer. Sometimes, also, it

*Quoted by Ben J. Wattenburg in *This U.S.A.* (New York: Doubleday, 1965).

19

requires outside help, the guidance and support of a skilled counsellor.

In this book I am going to act as your premarital counsellor. Of course it can't be a real counselling situation, because that requires face-to-face meetings and two-way communication. However, we shall do as much as we can to set up the conditions of a series of marriage preparation interviews. I suggest that we do this in three ways:

1. I will talk over with you the areas I would try to cover if you (I am thinking of two of you, a thinking-of-getting-married couple) had in fact come to me for marriage preparation as hundreds of couples have come to me through the years. I will raise with you the questions about yourselves, your relationship, your hopes and fears, your plans and expectations that I would talk over with you if we were actually meeting together.

2. You can't talk back to me, but you can talk to each other. And this is what I would want you to do. Either you could read each section of the book together, stopping as you go along and discussing whatever seems to apply to your particular personal lives, or you could each read a section separately in advance, recording anything you ought to talk over with each other – either by underlining it in the book or by making notes on a separate sheet of paper. Your discussion should take place in a leisurely setting, if possible in a secluded place where you are not likely to be interrupted.

3. If you become aware of areas in which you need help, you should find someone whom you both respect and trust to act as your counsellor. I have prepared a special appendix to this book to help you to find a competent

counsellor. It could be a minister, a marriage counsellor, or some other professional person qualified to give you the kind of help you want. In some special areas you might get most help from a doctor, a lawyer, or a financial counsellor. There might be some questions that could best be talked over – separately or together – with a trusted friend in your own age group or a married couple in whom you have confidence.

There are other ways in which the book might be used. Your minister or a marriage counsellor may have given you a copy as a means of helping you to identify and focus on the areas of your relationship where you specially need his help before taking your list to him as a basis for discussion.

Another possibility I would strongly recommend is that you might get into a marriage preparation group. For some years now we have realized the great help a group of couples can give to one another. They are travelling together over the same stretch of the same road, and this gives them a great deal in common. If any such programme is being offered in your community, I would urge you to join it. And if you can find nothing of the kind, you might even get together a group yourselves, or with the help of your minister. The group could then agree to read certain sections of this book in preparation for each of its weekly meetings. Couples thinking about marriage and recently married couples mix well for this purpose, and one advantage is that the married couples can invite the group to meet in turn in their homes.

What I am trying to emphasize is that the purpose of this book is to do something very practical – with you and for you. For this reason, I will write very much in the way I would talk, avoiding all involved and technical language, and all speculative and theoretical ideas. We will try to stick to the facts — and to the down-to-earth facts that are important to you, a couple moving toward marriage. So, we are ready to begin.

2 The Case for Marriage Preparation

The Boy Scout motto is 'Be Prepared'. It is an excellent idea to help boys (and girls too, of course) to learn early in life skills that will be useful to them later. This is in fact the main purpose of education. The school prepares us for a life vocation, and for the duties and responsibilities of citizenship. The church prepares us for living with a purpose. Our homes, if they are good ones, give us values, standards, and ideals.

The major area of life for which we are most poorly prepared is, unfortunately, marriage and family living. Yet for most of us this is the area in which we may find, if we are successful, our deepest happiness and fulfilment. I once asked a group of men, selected at random, what they would do if they had to choose between two packages – a congenial job and an unhappy home, or a happy home and an uncongenial job. After thinking it over, most of them said, 'Give me the happy home, and I'll put up with the job.' I didn't bother to take my question to a group of women. I knew what their answer would be.

So preparation for marriage is preparation for the one experience in life on which our happiness most deeply depends. In this chapter I want to spell this out in greater detail. Let us consider five of the major gains that marriage preparation can bring you:

1. *You will understand clearly what marriage means, and how to go about it.* Imagine two explorers setting off to make a journey through unknown territory. One has a map and compass, the other has neither. Which one is likely to find his way

through?

You may say, of course, that marriage is not unknown territory. We see marriages all around us, and we know what the functions of husbands and wives are. But in fact we don't see marriages. All we see is the façade the couple present to the world. What goes on between them in the intimate life they share is hidden. One of the things most couples don't generally do in our culture is to talk about what goes on in their relationship, and especially about anything that disturbs them. Their every instinct is to conceal their conflicts and turn a brave and smiling face to the world. You know how often, when a marriage breaks up, friends and even relatives will exclaim, 'This is so unexpected. We thought they were getting along fine.'

The evidence is overwhelming that most couples go into marriage with quite inadequate understanding of the roles of husband and wife. Marriage counsellors never cease to be amazed at the ignorance about marriage which they find in people otherwise well informed. There are at least two explanations of this. The first is that there is no clearly agreed time in life – at home, in school, in church, or anywhere else – when we give young people careful teaching about marriage. The second is that there is a persistent idea around that no special knowledge is needed in order to live together as a married couple. 'It comes naturally', people say. This is a serious illusion. The life of marriage is very complex, very demanding; the number of those who fail should be enough to make that clear. The sooner we face this undeniable fact the better.

So the prepared couple will have a great advantage over the couples who have not made themselves ready. They will understand what marriage involves, what adjustments have to be made. More important, they will have taken a good look both at themselves and at each other as persons, and they will know what they have to work with. They will understand the roles they have to play.

As I wrote some years ago in a foreword to Dr Henry Bowman's excellent book *Marriage for Moderns*, 'It is ridiculous to say, or to imply, that those who have learned something of the art of achieving a good marriage relationship will be no better off than those who know nothing about it.'

2. *You will be able to make the critical early adjustments of marriage smoothly and quickly.* Motor mechanics tell us that the way a car is treated in the first thousand miles will have a deep and lasting influence on the way it behaves later. Something like that is true also of the marriage relationship. We now know that the shape of a marriage develops quite early. In the first six or twelve months a couple develop habits of behaving toward one another that become settled and are not easily changed later. These habits decide a number of important questions: who plays the dominant and who the submissive role, who takes major responsibility for the different areas of the couple's shared life, how quarrels are handled, who initiates the first move to make up, who makes the final decisions in what areas, how household chores are allocated, how money is managed, how sexual needs are met, relationships with in-laws or former friends or neighbours, how leisure time is spent. These are just a few of the many areas in which patterns are developed in the early months of marriage. We shall discuss most of them in more detail later.

It is obvious that the way in which these patterns develop will have a great influence on the future of the marriage. Develop a set of good patterns, and the marriage will be off to a promising start. Drift into unsatisfactory and destructive ways of interacting in these areas, and the seeds are sown that will lead to all kinds of later trouble and conflict.

The unprepared, who have not thought about these matters, will allow patterns to develop in an unplanned, haphazard fashion. The prepared will try to do better. I am not suggesting, of course, that you can make an intellectual decision about how you will live together, and then just go ahead and carry it out. We are influenced in the way we behave by the habits of a life-time, and by the time we reach the age of marriage we can change ourselves only to a limited extent. Nevertheless, I have been convinced by my own experience as a marriage counsellor that a genuine willingness on the part of husband and wife to understand each other, to recognize the need for change, and to make sincere attempts to change as far as possible, can in most cases result in a very satisfying degree of mutual adap-tation. I am also convinced that it is much easier to do this in the early months of marriage than to try to do it later when habit patterns have become set, and when the motivation to make changes has run down.

3. *You will have a better chance of reaching higher levels of marital fulfilment.* Human relationships, as we are coming to understand them today, are very complex mechanisms. A marriage is perhaps the most complex of all because husband and wife live in the closest and most intimate of all adult relationships, and they play a great many roles and interact at a great many different levels.

What this means is that the *potential* in a marriage is likely to be greater than the couple ever realize. They can settle for any one of a wide range of levels. Some married couples live very superficially together. They communicate about routine matters, but do not share their deepest thoughts. They live almost separate lives under one roof. They meet each other's elementary needs but never venture into what I call relationship-in-depth. Surprisingly enough, they may never even really get to know one another, because all they reveal is a limited area of their true selves. They simply live together on the basis of a mutual exchange of services. He 'brings home the bacon', she takes care of the house, she gives him sex, he gives her children. Based on a few such elementary exchanges, the marriage soon becomes dull and dreary.

Such mediocre marriages are very common in our culture. Yet often these very people are tormented by the longing for a relationship that is richer, deeper, and more meaningful. They are love-starved, and often they turn in other directions to seek what marriage has failed to give them. The wife may become almost completely preoccupied with her children, the husband gets immersed in his job, either or both may turn to extra-marital affairs in the effort to find more satisfying love experiences.

Any couple who choose in marriage to develop their full potential and to seek relationship-in-depth will need to prepare and to work hard in the early years of their life together. For the making of a really good marriage is seldom brought about by chance. Like any other work of art, it is the result of informed, purposeful striving and creative effort.

4. *You will increase your chances of being successful parents.* Nowadays, many people fail to realize seriously the qualitative relationship between marriage and parenthood. The two are very intimately bound up together.

Physically, it is easy for any man and woman to bring about the conception of a child. They do not even have to know each other, let alone have a significant relationship. But once the child is conceived, the woman can adjust to pregnancy much better if she is sustained and supported by her child's other parent. And when the child is born, he needs increasingly the support and guidance both of his father and of his mother.

All this we know well. It is one of the major purposes of marriage. But what we fail to stress is that as the child grows up his need is not simply for two parents, but for *two parents who love each other* and love him as an expression and exten-sion of their love for each other. It is their mutual affection that creates the atmosphere that gives him emotional security.

It is their united faith in him that shapes his sense of purpose for his own life.

Of all the gifts which parents can offer to a child of their love, therefore, the greatest is that of a happy marriage. For this guarantees that he will be surrounded by the united love of both of his parents. In their pattern of discipline they will support each other, so that his world will be one of coherent order. Their goal for him will be fully shared. And because they find their love needs richly fulfilled in each other, they will be able to bestow on him a love that makes no adult demands which he cannot meet. Because they are not in conflict, he will not be inwardly torn by the need to struggle with a divided loyalty.

I once wrote an article with the title, 'Be Happily Married – For Your Children's Sake'. My plea was, that even if a married couple won't make the effort to work at their marriage for the rewards it can bring *them*, they should consider doing so for the rewards it can enable them to offer their children. This would apply equally to preparation for marriage. If you don't feel inclined to make the effort for the sake of your own future happiness, then make it for the sake of the happiness of your children yet unborn.

5. *You will understand the wisdom of seeking marriage counselling in good time if you ever come to need it.* One of the exasperations of the marriage counsellor is that people often delay coming to him for help until it is too late for much to be done. By the time they come, they have built up attitudes of hostility and resentment that have almost destroyed their love and poisoned their relationship. Sometimes, they have already found ways of escape from each other and have developed new love relationships outside marriage. To help such people is difficult, and it means sometimes an impossible task.

People who have sought preparation for marriage have more sense. They are less likely, of course, to get into trouble. But if

28

they do encounter serious conflict that they can't resolve by their own unaided efforts, they know what this means. They realize that there is no time to be lost, that they must get help before the destructive process of degeneration sets in and they begin to be progressively alienated from each other. They are enlightened enough to realize that marital health, like physical and mental health, must be closely watched, and professional help sought as soon as there are signs of possible serious trouble.

Summary

I hope I have convinced you that a strong case can be made for marriage preparation. Not only your own happiness as a couple, but also the happiness of your children, and quite possibly of other people as well, may depend upon it. Those who have prepared for marriage increase their chances of avoiding needless misery, of moving more quickly into the rich fulfilments that marriage has to offer, and of reaching a deeper quality of relationship than they might otherwise be able to achieve.

It makes sense, doesn't it?

3 Marriage as It Is Today

Before we begin to talk about you as a particular and very special couple, we ought to be sure that we understand marriage in our contemporary world – what it demands, what it offers, and how different it is from marriage in the past.

Outwardly, marriage seems to be the same now as it always was. Two people, a man and a woman, come together and enter into a shared life. Together they create a new unit of human society. They set up a home, children are born to them, and they establish what we call a family. Husband and wife have their own special tasks, but they cooperate to help and support each other, and they work together to bring up their children as useful members of the community. In due course, their children reach the age at which they are ready to marry, and the cycle of life goes on into another generation. Marriage is the foundation stone of the family, just as the family is the foundation stone of the community.

This has been the way in which most human beings have lived their lives for as far back as we can trace human history. And it has been the pattern of all known human societies throughout the world. The details have varied – in some cultures a man has been allowed more than one wife at a time, occasionally a woman has had more than one husband. But the broad pattern has never been changed.

Some people today talk about the family as an outworn institution, and even say that yours may be the last generation that will accept marriage. These are statements that are not supported by the facts. We have no convincing evidence that marriage and family life will not continue in the future as they have continued since human life began; if only because there is no other way we know of to provide satisfactorily for the needs men and women meet in each other, and for the all-important task of passing on to children what they require in order to take over the task of safeguarding our human values and maintaining our human culture. Many experiments have been made throughout human history to find alternatives to marriage and family life. None of them has endured for long.

However, if marriage is not in danger of extinction, it is certainly undergoing some profound changes which need to be clearly understood by every modern couple. The changes in marriage simply reflect the changes in our society, as we move from a rural-agricultural to an urban-industrial way of life. It isn't only marriage that is changing today, everything is changing. Conservative older people find this very disturbing. They want to sit still where they have always sat; but to their annoyance, they find themselves carried along on a vast conveyor belt, travelling to an unknown future. This not only annoys them, it alarms them. The mood of such people was well expressed by the title of a play that ran some years ago in London and New York, 'Stop the World, I Want to Get Off'.

Change, however, need not be threatening. On the whole, our human lot today is better than it has ever been in the whole of our long history. At least the means to enjoy 'the good life' are ours as never before; what we do about it depends on ourselves. This is equally true of marriage. It is possible for more people today to have better marriages than people have ever had at any previous time. The changes, when they are properly understood, are favourable to marriage at its best.

The heart of the change is summed up in the subtitle of a

book written by one of the most distinguished sociologists who has studied the family in this century, Dr Ernest W. Burgess. The phrase he used to describe the trend in marriage was 'From Institution to Companionship'.

We can clearly see the changes now taking place in three significant areas of marriage.

The Founding of a Marriage

In the past, marriage was first and foremost a social obligation. Setting up families and having children was essential to the survival of the tribe or community. So marriages were planned and arranged by the elders; or at least, the approval of the elders was needed before the couple were allowed to marry. When married, they usually lived with the husband's parents, or at least nearby on the family land. They were supervised and guided by their in-laws, because they would ultimately take on the task of caring for the family property, maintaining the family traditions, and continuing the family name and line through their children. So the ideal was that a boy married a girl from a neighbouring farm, who had been educated in the same school, had attended the same church, and whose parents shared the same political opinions as his own parents.

Nowadays, this has changed. People choose their own marriage partners, and parents have very little say in the choice. People often meet their future husbands and wives away from their home community, in college or at work in another city. Husband and wife may come from different religions, from different social backgrounds, even be of different race. One may have been raised in the country, the other in the city. One may come from a poor home, while the family of the other may be comparatively wealthy. They may hold very different views on many subjects and even have very different values and standards.

When modern people marry, they don't necessarily settle near their parents. Often they start out alone in a community where both are a long way from home. They do have the telephone to enable them to keep in touch, and visits back to the home community are easier to make nowadays. But most of their time will be spent with friends and neighbours whose customs and traditions are likely to be very different from those of their childhood home. And perhaps they won't stay long with those new friends and neighbours.

Clearly these new circumstances make marriage more difficult in a number of ways. Differences in customary ways of running the home, spending the money, fulfilling the roles of husband and wife, father and mother, will cause confusion, and major adjustments will be needed before the couple can settle down happily together. 'That wasn't the way I was taught to act' will become a familiar phrase, and each time it is said there will be a real possibility of conflict. Far more adjustments are needed to enable a marriage of this kind to succeed, than for a couple who begin with a common cultural background. This is abundantly demonstrated by the fact that sociological studies have discovered again and again that the most stable marriages are those between partners who have come from the same or similar communities. Other things being equal, the more diversity there is in cultural, religious, and racial backgrounds, the tougher is the task of overcoming the difficulties and making the marriage work.

The Marriage Partnership

We have been speaking of marriage in relation to its social environment. But when we look into the relationship between husband and wife, here also there have been tremendous changes.

33

In human history it seems that marriage has often produced undesirable conflict. In the older cultures, disturbances were avoided by two special devices. One was to decide in advance which of the two would be boss. Needless to say, it was always the husband! In the Orient, the duty of the wife was made perfectly clear; she must obey her husband in all matters. He made the major decisions, she accepted them. So there was no clash of conflicting wills, and peace reigned in the home. It was the woman, of course, who paid the price.

The other way of avoiding conflict was to separate the duties of husband and wife so that they didn't come into collision with each other. Generally speaking, the wife's sphere was in the home. The husband was responsible for the outside work, together with a few jobs in the house that required greater physical strength or mechanical skill. So they had their separate spheres of influence, and didn't interfere unduly with each other.

Today all this is changed. Women have been emancipated. Today's couple think of marriage as an equal partnership in which both share. Decisions are no longer made on a one-vote system; both partners have equal votes. The line between man's work and woman's work still exists, but it is becoming less and less clear. The wife of today, who holds a responsible job outside the home and may earn an income that is equal to that of her husband, is simply not prepared to be a meek little mouse, doing what she is told and subjecting her will to her husband's pleasure.

All this results in far more confusion and conflict than was likely in the marriage of the past. A two-vote system is much harder to operate than a one-vote system. Again and again the votes may be equally split. Then the issue must be decided by negotiation, which can be a long-drawn-out and complicated process. If the wife puts in an eight-hour day outside the home, it is hardly fair to expect her in addition to deal with all the household chores. So, because the modern wife is emancipated, the modern husband must be domesticated.

In today's marriages there are fewer and fewer stereotyped patterns. The roles of husband and wife have to be decided to meet their particular personal situation. As Dr Joseph Folsom once put it, the first thing the modern married couple needs to do is to draw up a constitution for their life together, to decide who does what, when and how. This makes much greater demands on both, and in consequence it is much easier for the marriage to become deadlocked.

Of course, marriage that is a truly equal partnership between husband and wife can be very rewarding. It provides a relationship in which each can freely contribute his or her gifts to the common welfare, and so develop a deep and satisfying comradeship. The modern marriage, therefore, offers greater possibilities of mutual satisfaction, but at a far higher price than before. It is not really surprising that many become disillusioned and give up the attempt.

The Task of Parenthood

The primary function of marriage has always been to produce children. In many cultures, a childless marriage is simply dissolved; it has failed to work. 'Be fruitful and multiply' is the best-known injunction the Bible gives to married people. And in the past it has been necessary to have many children in order to preserve the family and tribe. In some parts of the world, even today, as many as half of all children born die in their first year of life, and many who survive die before reaching maturity. So, the people argue, you must have many children to be sure of rearing a few who can take over the family's duties and look after their ageing parents.

Now this also has changed completely. Having many children

today doesn't ensure our survival. If all couples had large families, we are told we would soon be facing disaster. So the small family is the order of the day. In some ways, this certainly makes less work. But in other ways, it puts new responsibilities on the shoulders of the parents. In big families, older children took care of the younger, and often they solved each other's problems. Now each child needs a great deal of special individual care from his parents. He may need, too, a much more extensive education before he is ready to be a responsible adult. And he grows up in a society where he may challenge what his parents teach him and even rebel against them.

Modern patterns of child-rearing, therefore, have to be different. In the old days, the aim was to produce an obedient child who would accept his parents' authority, believe everything they said, and do what he was told. 'Little children,' it was often said, 'should be seen and not heard.' They were not expected to have opinions of their own; and even when they did have opinions, they were not encouraged to express them. Under those conditions, the task of parenthood was fairly manageable.

Today, that kind of parenthood doesn't work any more. Modern children grow up in an open society where they enjoy a degree of personal freedom quite unknown in the past. Obeying elders won't get them very far, because the elders disagree about what is good and right. For today's parents, the task of child-rearing is to co-operate with the child and teach him to make wise decisions, to use freedom with responsibility. This is a far more complex task, and requires of parents that they be enlightened, mature, infinitely patient, and above all united. This in turn makes great demands on marriage. Large numbers of married couples today are burdened with an oppressive sense of having failed as parents and are weary and heartsick about it. There is no evidence as yet that parenthood is getting any easier.

Summary

What this all adds up to is the fact that marriage today is no longer the comparatively easy process of following a standard blueprint. Each individual marriage has a character of its own, and presents the couple with a disconcerting array of difficult tasks to be performed if the goal of a happy and harmonious family life is to be achieved. Yet at the same time, marriage today has much to offer in terms of individual fulfilment and personality development and in emotional security, which the more rigid and stable marriages of the past often failed to make possible. There have, of course, been very happy marriages at all periods of our human history. Yet I would repeat that the chances of achieving very high levels of fulfilment are better today, for more people, than ever before.

The rewards are great, but the task is difficult. The moral is, be prepared.

2 *Yourselves*
what you bring to each other

4 How Well Do You Know Yourself?

Let me explain what we are going to do in this section of the book. First, I am going to ask each of you to look at yourself – who you are, how you came to be what you are, where you stand now, and what you are asking of life. Second, I shall invite you both to share with each other, as far as you feel able, what you have come to know and understand about yourselves. Third, I shall suggest that you discuss what it might mean to you as a couple to spend the rest of your lives together in the most intimate, and the most demanding, of all human relationships.

These are exactly the steps I would want you to take if you were coming to me for marriage preparation interviews. I would spend at least one hour with each of you separately, going over what we call your personal history. As you responded, I would make notes. After I had seen each of you separately, I would make an appointment for both of you to come together. Before I met with you, I would sit down with my notes and think about you, trying to picture you married to each other. I would consider what were the strengths in your relationship, the areas in which you would be in agreement, in which you would naturally support and fortify each other. Then I would consider the areas in which you would probably disagree or find yourselves in conflict (there are always some of these, even in the very well-matched couples).

When we sat down all together, I would encourage you yourselves to try to identify your strong points and your likely conflict areas, and I would check your impressions against my own. I could easily find that my estimates were wrong and had to be modified. After all, I would only have spent about an hour with each of you. But I might find, also, that I had spotted some things in your relationship that you had been unaware of, or at least things you had preferred not to think about or to face up to. We would talk together about all these matters during one or more interviews, taking whatever time proved to be necessary.

Let me make my aim very clear. I want you to come out of this experience with as clear a picture as you can obtain of yourselves as a couple. Why? Because it is far better to come to terms with the realities now than to be rudely awakened to them later. One reason for this is that you would obviously feel cheated later if you discovered important things about each other that you should have known before. Such an experience can produce bitterness and resentment, and feelings of that kind don't provide the right atmosphere for the adjustments that then have to be made.

The other reason for getting a clear picture of each other before marriage is that a great many of the adjustments you will have to make can begin during the pre-marriage period. In fact, one of the most worthwhile uses you can make of the months before your marriage is to get to know each other really well. Not all the serious conflicts you may have to face in marriage will necessarily emerge before you become man and wife, yet it is probable that you will become vaguely aware of most of them at one time or another in the early period of your acquaintance. As a couple looking toward marriage you can do a great deal of growing together, and this is in fact the best possible way of preparing for your future.

Many people think of marriage preparation as learning about marriage now so as to be able, when the time comes, to handle the various adjustments that will have to be made later to sex, to money, to in-laws, and so on. It is quite true that knowledge about these matters will be valuable to you, and ideally every couple should have such knowledge. However, the real purpose of this knowledge is not to tuck it away at the back of your mind for future use, but to make use of it now. Already you are coping, at least in a preliminary way, with most of the issues that will come up in full force when you become husband and wife. You are already dealing with sex, money, and in-laws; and the way you manage them now will provide the guidelines for handling them later.

In other words, marriage is not going to change the relationship that is already developing between you, but will only intensify it by enabling it to be more intimate, more continuous, and more demanding. So the best way in which you can prepare for your future marriage is to learn to be, here and now, a really successfully functioning couple. Your present, if it is well and wisely handled, will in many respects decide your future. Every successful adjustment you make to each other now will be a bonus that you can carry over into the next stages of your growth as a couple.

I am well aware that this idea of working on your relationship now may raise problems for you. One is a reaction I have often encountered. As one girl put it, 'This is a very special time in our lives, which we want to enjoy to the full. Looking at ourselves in the way you suggest is like questioning our love for each other. I'm afraid it might spoil the romance.'

I understand this anxiety. But the argument simply doesn't stand up. If you are just dating for fun, you don't need to get to know each other in depth. But when you are thinking seriously of marrying you simply have to face the facts, and it is quite irresponsible to refuse to do so. As to the argument that it would spoil your romance, that depends entirely on what you mean to each other. If you are still at the stage of projecting on each other your adolescent dreams of fairy princes and princesses, I have to tell you plainly as your counsellor, even at the risk of offending you, that it is now time to wake up, to exchange the land of dreams for the world of reality.

Your love for each other must be tested at this time. And if you truly love each other, knowing each other better will strengthen that love, not weaken it. As a matter of fact, one of the results of love between a man and a woman is a tremendous interest in each other that makes them want to know each other better and better. If you don't have this urge, perhaps you need to ask yourself whether after all you are only 'in love with love'.

Another problem I may have raised for you was expressed in this way by John, 'I frankly don't like this idea of telling Peg all about myself. There are some things I would rather keep to myself. She isn't the first girl I have gone around with, you know. And if I told her some of the things that happened with the others, we might break up. I am not prepared to risk that.'

What should people do about confessions? This boy naturally wanted to make the best possible impression on the girl he hoped to marry. That is what we all do during courtship, just as the male bird spreads his feathers before the female to show her what a fine fellow he is. However, as courtship leads on to marriage, the truth is that you can't successfully conceal your real self from the one you love, and it becomes more and more of a strain to try to do so.

In marriage we have to accept each other as we are. The failure to do this only leads to trouble. So if John is trying to hide from Peg something of himself which she will discover sooner or later, it's best to let her know now and take the consequences. People should go into marriage knowing all the really relevant facts about each other. If you can't begin your life together in honesty, the chances that you will ever develop a deep trust in each other are pretty poor.

However, this doesn't mean that John has to report to Peg in detail all the things he did, sexually and otherwise, with his previous girl friends. This might be quite an upsetting experience for Peg, and she would probably prefer not to hear such details.

I offer you a simple rule about confessions. If you feel you must make them, and you are quite sure you can do so in a loving way that won't cause distress to your partner, go ahead. But if you are in doubt about it, follow this plan. Go first and make the confession in full to someone you respect and trust, and discuss whether it would be good to make the confession to the one you plan to marry. If the decision on which you both agree is not to do so, you should find that the matter won't worry you any further. You have shown your willingness to tell, and that is what matters most. If at some later time the facts should come out, and your marriage partner asks you why you didn't confess before, your reply is that you were quite willing to do so, and that you *have* in fact told someone (whom you could name). You then explain that you withheld the confession from your partner, because it seemed at the time to be the most loving thing to do.

Now we should be ready to begin, if you are willing. We will start with each of you separately. Since I can't be actually present with you to take notes, I suggest that you get a pencil and paper and put down, as we look at your personal history, whatever you think is important. Then you can each go over your notes carefully, take a good look at yourself and decide how to present the results of your individual thinking to the other.

There is another way to do this, and you may prefer it. Let me tell you how one couple went about it. There was a parking place on a hill, from which they could gain a commanding view of the city where they lived. On a succession of evenings, they drove to this spot. They took it in turns to tell their life stories to each other, just everything about their earlier lives they could think of. They finally reached a point at which each was able to say to the other, 'Now I'm finished. You know as much about me as I know about myself.' According to their testimony, they found the experience a very rewarding one.

The method doesn't matter. What does matter is that any two people who plan to spend their whole lives together ought to know each other pretty well at the start. If there is any time in life at which you could with profit take a long, hard look at yourself, surely it is just before you entrust your life and happiness to another.

5 What Made You What You Are?

The traditional challenge of the sentry is, 'Halt! Who goes there?' Before being allowed to pass, you must identify yourself. So it should be with marriage. Before being allowed in, you should identify yourself to yourself and to your partner.

But how does a person identify himself? It can be done at two very different levels. The first is to describe oneself on the outside in terms of labels: age, education, job, religion, politics, and so on. But that doesn't identify the real you, the kind of person you are, any more than your photograph does. Despite the film caricatures, in real life it is impossible to tell heroes from villains by their looks. If I listed your general description in terms of the labels you wear and published it with the offer of a thousand pounds if this person would come forward, I would probably have quite a number of applicants to deal with. There would be honest and dishonest people, generous and mean people, responsible and irresponsible people, all answering your general description.

The other way of identifying yourself is by association with another person, in which you open up your inner self and reveal the kind of person you really are. Of course, this is what is important in marriage. It is what you are like inside and how you are likely to relate to the person to whom you are closest in the world, that matters.

In this chapter, I am inviting you (each of you separately) to take a good look at yourself. This is not an easy thing to do.

Self-assessment can be unreliable, because you have built up defences against recognizing some realities about yourself which you would rather not acknowledge. Many people don't accept themselves as they are; they try desperately to appear before the world as other than they are. They try to appear more honest, more educated, more handsome (with the aid of clothes and makeup), more pleasant (by concealing their ill temper). In fairly superficial relationships this pays off, and we all do it to some extent.

In the intimate life of marriage, however, this just isn't going to work. There our pretences are stripped away, and we appear before each other as we really are. Therefore, since you are looking at yourself now as a candidate for marriage, it must be an honest look at the real you because that's the person your partner is going to live with.

The best way to know yourself as you are is to understand the forces that have shaped your personality. You didn't make yourself. You came into the world with certain basic endowments. But you became what you are now as a result of the way in which you reacted and adapted to the conditions under which you lived and to the people you had to get along with. So let us look now at these major influences in your life and what they have made of you.

For convenience, we shall divide up your personal history into nine aspects.

Your Family Background

This aspect is by far the most important, and we could spend a lot of time on it. Up to now, your parents have almost certainly been the most influential people in your life. Your basic endowment came either from them or through them from earlier ancestors. They shaped your life almost exclusively in your formative early years, and they have probably continued

48

to have a deep and powerful influence over you. Most of your ways of behaving have been either copied from them consciously or unconsciously, or have developed out of your rebellion against them.

Look now, therefore, at your parents. What was your basic relationship to each of them? Were you close to both of them? To one, but not the other? To neither of them? By closeness, I mean warmly expressed love, affection, and trust. A good test is to ask how far you felt able to confide in them.

Closeness to parents is good in the childhood years. But if that closeness continued in your teen years so that it was difficult for you to free yourself and establish your independence, did the closeness become dominance on your parent's side? That is not so good.

Another question to ask is, how did they rear you? Were you satisfied with the way in which you were disciplined? Did you feel you were well understood? Did you feel you received fair treatment? In general, patterns of discipline that are too severe or too lax harm the child. What is best for him is a pattern that is firm but fair.

Try to evaluate, also, their relationship to each other. A child sees in his parents a close-up demonstration of the way in which a man and a woman relate to each other, and that deeply influences his own expectations. His parents are his models. A boy learns from his father how a man treats a woman, and from his mother how a woman responds to her man. A girl likewise learns from her parents how the masculine and feminine roles are played.

A good way to evaluate the influence of your parents is to ask yourself, 'What things in the life of my parental home would I want to carry over into my own home, and what things would I not want to carry over?'

If you decide that you were the happy child of warm, loving parents with whom you enjoyed a close and confiding relationship, by whom you were not hindered in your growth to independence, and whose pattern of married love you would want to repeat in your own marriage, you have reason to feel fortunate. This, according to research findings, doubles your chances of successful marriage. If you came from an unhappy home, however, that does not condemn you to marital misery. It simply alerts you to the fact that you may have to work a bit harder than the average person to ensure success.

Your Social Adjustment

You have developed your own individual methods of relating to other people, and these will certainly affect the way in which you relate to your marriage partner. So you should try to understand your pattern of social adjustment.

As well as your parents, your brothers and sisters influenced you here. If you were an older child, you probably had to take some responsibility for the others. If you were the youngest in the family, you were probably indulged, though you may have been the one everyone picked on, too. If you were an only child, you probably felt important and got used to being in the centre of the whole picture, yet outside the family you could have found relationships difficult. These are only some of the patterns that develop. Try to decide what yours was.

Then look at your relationship to others outside the family. Did you have plenty of childhood friends, or were you lonely and withdrawn? How did you rank in the group of kids you played with? Did you take the lead? Or were you just one of the crowd, accepting what the others decided? Or did you feel inferior and inadequate?

As you grew up, how did you learn to react to other people in your life? Have you become confident and self-assured? Insecure and self-conscious? Or something in between? Do you react with apprehension or hostility when you meet new people for the first time? If so, do you express this openly, or try to conceal it behind a surface politeness? In your social circle, do you like the gay party atmosphere with plenty of people around? Or are you more at ease with a few trusted cronies? When you are upset and hurt, do you spill out your feelings or withdraw into yourself and avoid other people until you have recovered your composure?

It will be obvious to you that your answers to these and other similar questions will give you valuable clues about how you are likely to react to a very close and continuous relationship with a marriage partner. Try to assess your assets and liabilities in this important area.

Your Intellectual Development

How much formal education did you get? This will clearly determine to some extent the kind of people you like to talk with. A person much more ignorant than yourself would be apt to become boring. Someone who knew much more than you did could make you feel inferior.

Did you measure up, in school, to what your parents and teachers expected of you and to what you expected of yourself? If not, do you suffer from feelings of intellectual inadequacy in relating to other people so that you avoid discussions of matters you don't understand and are afraid to admit ignorance in case people will think you stupid? If you know you are not a highly intelligent person, have you accepted this comfortably, recognizing that you have other good qualities that your friends can appreciate?

Your Vocational Development

Have you found the kind of work you can do well and take pride in? Or are you restlessly trying to prove yourself to yourself and to others? To be contented and confident in your job is vital to your self-esteem and happiness. It may be vital also to the happiness of your partner. A person driven relentlessly by unsatisfied ambitions can be very difficult to live with.

Are you satisfied that your vocational plans can assure your family of economic security and provide you and them with what will be needed to live in reasonable comfort?

Your Spare Time Interests

Given a stretch of time with no commitments and no obligations, how would you choose to spend it? In other words, to what kind of activities do you naturally turn when all these outside pressures are off? The answer to this question can tell you a good deal about the kind of person you really are.

Do you tend, in such a situation, to seek the company of others, or to prefer seclusion? Are you motivated toward hobbies that enable you to compete successfully and to prove your worth? Or to creative enterprises that give you inward satisfaction? Or to escapist activities that enable you to forget your anxieties and responsibilities?

Your Spiritual Development

What does religion mean to you? Is it a matter of conforming to rules and customs you were brought up to obey? Or is it a matter of group loyalty, feeling that you belong to a company of people who give you a sense of security and support? Or is your religion a deeply personal source of strength and purpose in your life?

What is your basic philosophy of life? What are the standards of personal integrity you try to meet? How would you describe your fundamental goal in life? Is it essentially a quest for personal satisfaction and fulfilment? Or would you call yourself 'service-oriented'? Do you consider that both can be combined?

How does this affect your sense of your duties and obligations to others, especially those to whom you are closely related? Do you tend to use them for your own ends? How far can you find genuine satisfaction in making others happy? How far can you tolerate faults in other people, and be patient and understanding toward them? Does your caring for your friends extend to sacrificing your own immediate goals if necessary, in order to help them to achieve their goals?

Your Sexual Experiences

Would you say that you feel basically comfortable about your own sexuality? Or is this an area of your life that creates anxiety, guilt, or insecurity?

In your past, were you helped to develop an essentially positive feeling about sex as something good and healthy? Or was it experienced as part of yourself that was dirty, disreputable, or unwholesome? Did you have sexual experiences – masturbation, homosexuality, seduction, casual sexual encounters – that left you feeling hurt and disturbed?

If you have had experiences of pre-marital sexual intercourse, of what kind have they been? Were you persuaded into them against your better judgement? Did you go into them with a divided mind? Have they left you with a guilty conscience? Did they involve exploitation of those with whom you shared them?

Your approach to marriage can be deeply affected by skeletons in the cupboard in this area. If you are troubled about this, it might be of great help to go and talk it all over with a marriage counsellor.

Your Love Relationships

What have been your experiences of friendship with the opposite sex, of falling in and out of love? Have they been pleasant and carefree, enabling you to grow and find yourself? Have you been able to function as a loving, caring person? Or have you had difficulties in this area?

Apart from sex, have you been able to enjoy experiences of intimacy with people you have loved? Have you learned to share your deepest feelings with such people, and to be open about yourself? Have you found that you could handle awkward situations, differences of opinion, conflicts about each other's attitudes and behaviour, by talking things over honestly and so restoring the original mutual warmth and affection?

Have you had unpleasant, painful experiences in which you have been exploited or let down by people you loved and trusted? Have you yourself damaged your relationship with others by developing uncontrollable anger, frustration, hostility, or by finding yourself unable to cope with the tumult of your own feelings and having to break the relationship and escape from it?

Physical and Mental Health

What has been your health record? Have you had any serious illnesses or major accidents or operations? How have these affected you? Did they make you feel unable to achieve your goals? Did they cause you to be overprotected as a child? Do you have any disabilities that restrict you in any way from living a normal life or that would affect you as a marriage partner, or as a parent?

What about your mental health? Have you suffered from any kind of nervous or emotional breakdown? Was it satisfactorily cleared up, or could it recur under conditions of stress?

How would you describe your temperament? Are you on the whole a contented, cheerful person? Or do you tend to be often gloomy and depressed? Do you experience wide changes of mood, from enthusiasm to despair? Are there situations in which you are overwhelmed with dread or panic? Is your basic attitude to life one of self-confidence, or of fear and apprehension?

Summary

I have raised a great many questions about you as a person, and I could have raised a great many more. My suggestion is that you respond to these questions, and others that occur to you, by writing down your evaluation of yourself in these general areas. It is specially important to note any area that arouses anxiety or emotional tension in you and to try to discover why you are affected in this way. It will surely be clear to you why these aspects of your life may have a bearing on your future; the whole of what you are is going to be involved in the experience of sharing life totally with the one you love.

Your evaluation of yourself is your own. But I hope that you can share most of it with your future partner in a joint session. And if you find yourself confused or perplexed about any aspect of yourself that we have considered, it might save you a lot of unnecessary unhappiness, now and later, to get counselling help about it. Seeking help in understanding yourself is not a sign of weakness. It is a manifestation of wisdom and good judgement.

6 Where Are You Now?

I am assuming that you have both now taken a good look at yourselves, individually and separately, and have been able to follow this up by sharing your self-evaluations with each other. The next step is to look at yourselves, not separately but in combination, to make an evaluation of yourselves jointly as a couple moving toward marriage.

I should explain to you at this point that there are two distinct factors that influence success in marriage. One is the *marriage-ability* of each of the partners, the combination of qualities you individually possess that is favourable to good marital adjustment. It is at these qualities that we have been looking. But there is also another factor, perhaps of equal importance. This is your *compatibility*, how well you are suited, not to marriage generally, but to each other. We are now going to look at this, and it will be best for you to do it together.

The first obvious question to ask is, how did you two happen to move towards each other, to see in each other something good and attractive, and to develop your relationship to the point at which you now plan to marry?

You will never be able to answer that question fully, because it concerns a very complex process in which some deeply unconscious motivations in both of you have been at work. However, as far as it is possible to formulate your answer, you should try to do so.

Our Mate Selection System

In the old days, as we have seen, mate selection was often arranged by the parents. Now people make their own choices. In order to adjust to this change, we have evolved in our Western world a system of mate selection which, on the whole, is very sound, provided you work it properly. You might like to compare your own experience with the general pattern.

The system works in three stages. First, there is *random dating*, an arrangement to allow boys and girls to learn to be comfortable with each other socially. A boy and a girl may go out together for a pleasant evening and enjoy each other's company without any commitment on either side. This enables young people in early adolescence to get over any self-consciousness they may have in the presence of the opposite sex, to learn to talk and feel at ease with each other, and to get some idea of the kind of partner they get along with most happily and comfortably. Dating is used for other purposes than this, but this is the major argument in favour of it, and it is a pretty convincing one.

The second stage is what used to be called *courtship*, a deeper relationship between a boy and a girl who have found that they get along specially well with each other and are at this point more interested in getting to know each other better than in continued random dating. Often they will feel that they are in love, and they may talk at least tentatively about the possibility of marriage at some future time. But this stage involves no commitment. If, as they spend more time together, they seem after all not to be as well suited to each other as they at first thought, they will recognize this and break up. Parting may be temporarily a painful experience for one or for both, but recovery is usually quite rapid and complete.

If, however, the couple find, as they get to know each other better, that they do indeed have a great deal to give to each other, they may become more deeply involved in each other's lives; and if they feel they are old enough, they may now definitely decide to marry. This is the third stage, generally called *engagement*. Traditionally it has meant that the boy gives the girl a ring, as an outward token that they are definitely planning to marry, and often a tentative date is now set for the wedding. This means a definite commitment on the part of both. But if, as time passes, they begin to have serious doubts about whether to go on to marriage, they can break the engagement. At this stage, a break may be quite painful and embarrassing, but it is far better to end an engagement when real doubts arise than to go on into a marriage that might end in disaster.

This mate selection system is a good one – in fact, I cannot imagine anything better. Each stage can be a learning process. At each stage the quality of the relationship is tested, and at each stage it can be terminated if it fails to measure up to the test. Properly used, this system should give most people a good chance to find a compatible marriage partner. Unfortunately it is not always properly used. Some couples, at the time when they should be asking serious questions about their marriage prospects, avoid this altogether and give themselves little opportunity to explore the interpersonal levels of their relationship. Other couples, although they have deep misgivings about each other, ignore these warnings, taking refuge in such reassuring statements as, 'It will all come right after we get married' or 'When we settle down together, I can change him.' Needless to say, these hopes are seldom fulfilled.

I recommend you to share together your personal experiences with the mate selection process as I have outlined it. Are you reasonably sure that you are being realistic in your judgements about your suitability to each other? Are there any areas of serious doubt or uncertainty that you should talk over with a counsellor?

Sociological studies, as we have seen, have shown that a good deal of compatibility in marriage is based on the fact that the couple came to each other with much in common. The general rule is that the more differences there are, the more adjustment they will have to make to each other. Let us look at some of the areas where difference could involve hazards.

Age: Modern marriages seem to work best for those who are about the same age, because this makes it more likely that their interests will be similar. An age difference in which the man is a few years older than the woman is the favoured pattern, though a difference of up to as much as ten years may not cause problems. Likewise, marriages in which the wife is up to about five years older work well nowadays. Differences much greater than these should be looked at very carefully. There would need to be a lot of compensating advantages to justify such unions.

Social differences can bring strains. Being married to someone whose personal habits are very different from those you have accepted as normal can be exasperating, and if neither partner is comfortable with the relatives and friends of the other, this can also lead to serious complications.

Wide *educational differences* work in very much the same way. This can be specially troublesome when the wife is much better educated than her husband. If she corrects his grammar and emphasizes his ignorance, he is likely to react with hostility.

What about religious differences? Interfaith marriages are common enough these days, and many of them succeed. Yet if the basic beliefs and loyalties of the couple are divided, a marriage will always tend to fall short of the ideal of 'one heart, one mind'. Problems can easily arise between the two families, particularly when there is conflict about the religious teaching of the children. Other things being equal, the inter-faith marriage presents greater hazards, and is more likely to fail, than the union of two people of the same faith. This is equally true of a marriage between a deeply religious person and a partner who treats religion with indifference or contempt.

Inter-racial unions are increasing these days, though they still represent only a tiny minority of all marriages. Much evidence suggests that they involve special difficulties. When such marriages fail, this tends to confirm and support existing racial prejudices. It is probably best at the present time that such unions should take place only between very mature people who have the resources necessary to make them succeed.

What about common tastes? This matters much less than common standards. But of course the companionship of husband and wife will be enhanced if they have the same basic ideas about the kind of house they want to live in, the kind of leisure activities they enjoy, the kind of people they like to meet. Differences here, however, need not be destructive. There should be enough flexibility in any marriage to allow husband and wife to arrive at compromises on relatively nonessential matters, and now and then to go their separate ways.

As part of your preparation for marriage, I would recommend you to go over your areas of common interest, list them and see how much you can happily share together. Then focus on your areas of difference and disagreement, and find out how much enduring tolerance you can contribute to keeping the peace. All couples differ about some things, and this is not necessarily disastrous to a marriage. Where differences are many and deep, however, much tolerance is required.

What About Temperamental Differences?

People sometimes argue about whether married people get on best if they are alike, or whether there is something in the idea of the attraction of opposites. The truth seems to be that in good marriages we find both factors present. One formula which expresses this is 'cultural similarity and emotional complementarity'.

You will find it challenging, and I think fascinating, at this point to sit down together and ask each other: 'What were the special things that attracted you to me? What needs of yours did you hope I would be able to meet?' Try writing down your answers to these questions separately first, without any collaboration, and then compare notes. I usually take time to get a couple involved in this kind of discussion.

Sexual attraction usually comes up right away. Of course this is important for people planning to marry; without it, I couldn't advise them to go ahead. But it is not a basis for marriage in itself, and should therefore not be at the top of the list. If it is, see that it is adequately supplemented by plenty of other favourable factors, or you may find yourselves in trouble.

What about dominance and submission? Some women unconsciously look for a strong, masterful, masculine husband. And some husbands feel a need to act protectively toward a wife who has strong dependency needs. But tread warily here. Aggressive males are often far from strong, and many a woman has been deceived on that score. Also, a wife who wants to lean on her husband all the time may become an intolerable burden to him, because he also has dependency needs. These supposed masculine-feminine differences are largely cultural stereotypes which we are giving up today. The marriage that works best nowadays is not a combination of strength and weakness, but a flexible companionship in which the dominance-submission roles can be switched when necessary.

What about the extrovert-introvert combination? On the whole it isn't a good one, because the principle of complementarity doesn't really apply. A man who likes a quiet life will not be helped by a wife who wants to give parties all the time, and the wife who is a home-lover will languish if her husband spends all his evenings rushing from one committee to another. Two extroverts or two introverts usually find it easier to adjust to marriage, than a combination of both.

All the same, a strong factor in mate selection is the desire of each of you to be identified in some way with qualities in the other that you yourself seem to lack. It would be helpful to you both to understand how far this has contributed to bringing you together.

Acceptance and Tolerance of Each Other

What must be recognized is that living with each other's temperamental differences is one of the most difficult, and yet one of the most important, tests of a marriage. To be sensitive to each other's changes of mood, and where possible to be understanding and supportive, is the art of living together in harmony. All human beings suffer from fear and anger and self-distrust at times. And these are the testing times in a close relationship. If you can accept and support each other at such times, you will tend to grow closer together in mutual interdependence. If at such times you reject each other, you will tend to drift apart.

This acceptance and tolerance of each other is already being tested in you as a couple seriously considering marriage. Your interpersonal encounter with each other doesn't begin when you marry. You are involved in it right now. Your similarities and differences are already manifesting themselves, now pulling you toward each other, now generating experiences of coolness which drive you apart. What I am asking you to do is to examine these experiences together and try to understand them. It is not always possible to do this at the time, because feelings can get too strong to be calmly or rationally expressed. But recognizing the feelings you generate in each other is highly important for the understanding of what is going on between you, and the understanding of what is going on between you is highly important for the growth of a relationship of mutual love and trust.

Summary

Where are you now? Are you beginning to have some answers to this question? Can you now identify some of the things that are holding you together? Are there also things that are tending to drive you apart? All these need to be explored, understood, and dealt with if they call for appropriate action. This is the art of building a sound, wholesome relationship. You should find it stimulating and challenging. If you don't, maybe you need more help than you are able to give each other.

7 What Are Your Goals and Plans?

In the process of looking at yourselves, you may have noticed that we began with your past, the influences in your individual lives that have shaped you. Then we considered your present, what is now going on between you. In this chapter, we shall turn to your future, what lies before you as a couple planning to marry.

Examine Your Expectations

Let's begin with your expectations. You have each developed, through the years, a kind of fantasy picture of what it will be like to be married, the joys and fulfilments you hope for. Since a great many difficulties in marriage develop because expectations are not fulfilled, now is the time to take a look together at your two separate blueprints.

The best way to do this is for each of you, without collaboration, to write out a common statement on 'what I am expecting from our marriage'. It needn't be a long statement, but it should be quite specific. Vague generalities like 'I want us to be very happy' won't help. You must really get down to the practical details.

Now exchange these statements and plan a discussion session in which you can ask yourselves realistically how far your expectations are likely to be met. You'll probably have to do some revising of the blueprint. Some specifications will have to be altered, some scaled down, some even dropped (you will notice that I am likening this process to the joint building of your dream house, and it is rather like that).

Dreams and fantasies are all right. I believe in them. But we must be prepared to make concessions when we translate them into reality. This is particularly true of marriage, which we have idealized and romanticized to an excessive degree. As someone once expressed it, most of our complaints about marriage are based not on the fact that it is worse than the rest of human life, but that it is not infinitely better.

Some expectations, therefore, must be given up. Otherwise, you are going to be doomed to future disillusionment. However, to a reasonable extent, building castles in the air is all right. Thoreau said so – then he went on, 'That is where they ought to be. Now build the foundations under them.'

How do you do this? By setting your goals clearly, satisfying yourselves that they correspond to attainable reality, and then making plans to work progressively towards achieving them. To use the illustration of the dream house again, produce a blueprint on which you are both agreed, make sure that your particular house can be built on your chosen plot, and that the materials you would need for building it are available.

What Kind of Marriage for You?

In setting your goals, you will find yourselves having to decide what kind of marriage you really want. Marriages have been 'typed' in many different ways. For your practical needs right now, let's confine ourselves to the question of the extent to which you really want, or are really able, to become involved in the sharing of each other's lives.

Marriage offers you many levels of mutual involvement, and we can summarize them under three headings. There are the marriages of *minimum involvement*. I have already referred to these. Husband and wife enter into a kind of agreement to meet

65

each other's needs by an exchange of services. He promises to provide maintenance for her and their children on a basis that represents the accepted standard within their social group. He will also perform the general duties of a husband and father, but not to an extent that would seriously interfere with his vocational goals or his hobbies. She, for her part, agrees to be sexually available to him at all reasonable times, run the home, cook the meals, and bring up the children. Beyond that, she will be free to pursue her own interests and to cultivate her friendships with other women.

This kind of marriage is quite common in our culture. You could probably name many couples who function on this basis. They don't normally 'sign up' in advance for minimum involvement, and probably they are not even aware that this is the type of marriage they have chosen. But that is in fact what they have done, and they may be well satisfied. A marriage of this type makes few demands, and if this is all the husband and wife are expecting, there is a good chance that their expectations will be met.

In contrast with this is the marriage of *maximum involvement*. Idealistic couples may plunge eagerly for this, but they had better consider carefully what they are getting into. This is the marriage in which the couple decide to share their lives to the greatest possible extent. It implies a decision to live together in complete openness and honesty with each other, to devote themselves to working together for the same life goals, to attach equal importance to the personal needs and vocational aims of both partners, and not to favour one above the other. At the heart of this marriage lies the commitment to seek relationship-in-depth, the growth of the interpersonal relationship toward the realization, as nearly as possible, of its fullest potential.

It should be understood clearly that not many people are ready to pay the price of achieving this kind of marriage, nor does our culture favour it. Yet it is an ideal which some couples take seriously, and some – though only a few – attain it. Lederer and Jackson* estimate that only about five to ten per cent of all couples achieve this kind of completely satisfying marriage, and this would seem to me to be a reasonable estimate.

For most couples the likely goal lies somewhere between these extremes, a marriage of *limited involvement*. They want to retain a good deal of individual freedom to go their own ways, but also they wish to enjoy a reasonable amount of 'togetherness'. They are ready to be open to each other about most areas of their lives, but they want to reserve some territories which they do not share. They want to give the marriage a worthy place among their commitments, but are not prepared to award it the top priority.

What is important is that you as a couple should try to set your goals together in advance. You should plan a full discussion of this. Your goals needn't of course be rigidly set; you cannot know in advance what you are capable of achieving, but reaching some general agreement now could save you a lot of trouble later. The real tragedies occur when husband and wife, sometime after marriage, awaken to the realization that their goals and expectations for their life together, which they never really explored beforehand, turn out to be radically different and incapable of reconciliation. This is the time of disillusionment, of the shattering of the dreams.

The Inevitability of Conflict

It is as well to recognize at the beginning in choosing your marital goals, that the more involvement you decide for the more effort is going to be required to fulfil your expectations. The marriage of minimal involvement makes very few demands on you. The marriage of maximum involvement will demand

*William J. Lederer and Don D. Jackson, *The Mirages of Marriage*, p. 199.

all you've got. Up and down the scale, the rule is that the more closeness and intimacy you seek, the greater the price you'll have to pay to get it.

Social psychologists help us to understand this by looking at relationships in terms of distance. If we imagine marriage as a box containing two people, their difficulties in living comfortably together will depend upon the size of the box. If it is a mile square, they needn't get too much involved. In times of tension, they can easily get out of shouting distance of each other. However, if you reduce the box to ten yards square, the situation is greatly changed. Living in that kind of closeness, if you do things that irritate each other, the distress suffered will be great, and the pain won't stop until you find a way to reduce the irritation.

Why then make the box so small? Because it is closeness and intimacy that we want and need. This is the great gift which marriage has to offer us. Sharing life in depth with another person is the solution to most of our human problems. It is in loving and being loved that we find the real meaning of life. Yet in seeking the closeness and intimacy that this involves, we inevitably generate conflict. This is our central human dilemma.

What this means is that the more you want to get out of marriage, the more conflict you will have to resolve in order to get it. For closeness emphasizes our differences, increases the possibilities for disagreement, and generates the heat of conflict. It would be true to say that *no close relationship can be achieved and maintained in any other way than by resolving the conflict which it inevitably produces.*

At whatever level you set your marital goals, some conflict will have to be dealt with. You must be having some right now, as an engaged couple. It is true that some couples, having very flexible and tolerant dispositions, generate less conflict or are able to handle conflict much more easily than others; but it must also be recognized that the couples who have little conflict are not necessarily those who achieve the best marriages. A relationship free of conflict may be so because it is really a superficial relationship. Some of the best marriages I have ever encountered have been those of couples who have confided to me that they have been through seas of trouble – 'blood and sweat and toils and tears,' said one husband, quoting Winston Churchill. But he went on to say that the struggle they had been through together had not only enabled the conflicts to be resolved, but had also led them both to value deeply the good relationship they had achieved at so great a cost.

Communication and Co-operation

The task of achieving a good marriage will make many demands on you as a couple, and will probably require some years of effort. It should be effort highly rewarded, but this will happen only if you go about it in the right way. Some couples expend enormous effort in trying to deal with their problems of mutual adjustment, yet the effort is in vain, because they use the wrong methods.

There are two means that together provide the sovereign remedy for most of the ills of marriage. They are *communication* and *co-operation*. Both are needed, because neither gets us very far without the other; although, fortunately, each tends to facilitate the other.

I believe it would be true to say that the task of marriage counselling involves, very largely, working with married couples in trouble with the objective of improving their communication and increasing their co-operation. This sounds easy. In fact, it is often very difficult.

In a close relationship, two people are all the time acting on each other, reacting to each other, and interacting with each other. That is the very nature of relationship – messages, verbal and nonverbal, are shuttling back and forth all the time. As long as these messages are interpreted as pleasant and friendly and supportive, husband and wife are happy and all goes well. But as soon as something negative or critical comes over from your partner, you react, you feel pain, you tense up and become defensive, you probably send back a negative message expressing your disapproval. Your partner may have known that his original message was negative, so he is not surprised to get a negative response. But his negativeness may have hurt you much more than he expected, and the forcefulness of your response may hurt him so that he sends back a more strongly negative message than the last time. Or he may not even have known that his original message would be interpreted by you as negative, because he didn't intend it that way. He is therefore angry with you because you misjudged him. So back comes his expression of annoyance.

You must surely recognize what I am describing. This kind of negative exchange between two people can happen quite easily and can start quite innocently. If it is often repeated, it develops into what I call a negative interaction spiral – one negative message being hurled back in response to another, and the process repeated like an exchange of artillery fire. When a couple get embattled in this kind of destructive process, it can alienate them seriously from each other. It becomes impossible to tolerate closeness, and they move away from each other till they get out of earshot.

This leads to a total breakdown of communication, which makes the situation worse because there is no possibility of mutual explanation of how it all got started. In this state of distance and tension, any attempt to restore closeness can easily start off another negative interaction spiral. So the relationship degenerates from bad to worse.

The best way of avoiding this kind of destructive erosion of the relationship is to keep the lines of communication open. A negative exchange can be stopped if one partner, instead of firing back another salvo, can say, 'Look, we are in conflict. Can't we call a halt, calm down, and try to understand why we are doing this to each other?' This isn't easy, because angry people are not usually very rational. However, if the lines of communication are open, the first possible opportunity should be seized, after both have cooled down, to go over the whole experience, analyse what really happened, and take whatever action is needed to lessen the chance that the same thing will happen again.

What do I mean by 'keeping the lines of communication open'? I mean agreeing to share negative feelings whenever they arise, without bitterness if possible. For instance, you could say, 'Darling, you've done something that makes me furious, and I don't want to be angry with you. If I tell you about it, will you help me to understand just why I feel so hostile?' This may not always work, but it often will. The principle is, try not to swallow or bury any of your negative feelings (of which you will generate plenty) towards each other, but bring them out into the light of understanding. If all married couples learned to do just that, they would put most marriage counsellors out of action.

Keep Working Towards Your Goal

Honest communication opens the way for co-operation. This must follow. If you just unload your negative feelings, that will give you only temporary relief. It is necessary to probe the situation till you really understand it, and then to experiment together till you find the way to adjust to each other so that it can't happen again.

Whatever marriage goals you set, the way to realize them is to keep communicating. Tolerate no misunderstanding between you. Misunderstanding breeds resentment, resentment produces

71

hostility, and hostility starts the negative interaction spiral. Stop it at its source.

Nothing I can offer you will help you more than to learn the habit of examining your negative feelings to each other. Use your quarrels to practise this art. Go back over what happened, share with each other how you felt, discover the root of the difference between you, and find a way of digging it out. Do this over and over again in every negative exchange in which you become involved. Turn all your negative interactions into positive interactions. If you can do this, with or without counselling help, the goal of a mutually satisfying relationship is within your reach.

3 Marriage
what you must do to succeed

8 How to Live With Sex

If you were really making that trip to Africa, you would want to learn something in advance about where you were going. You'd study a map to see what the territory was like – mountains here, plains there, rivers flowing to the sea. You'd look at the political divisions on the map, the various countries and their capital cities. You would read a few books describing what life is like in Africa – the climate, the customs of the people, what to see, what to eat, what to wear.

In this section of our book we are going to do something like that. Preparing for marriage, as I have already stressed, is concerned less with facts than with feelings, with how you need to act rather than with what you need to know. But getting to know the facts is part of it too. So what I want to do at this point is to discuss with you some of the aspects of married life that give people trouble, and that you should know about in order to be prepared. All I can do in very limited space is to emphasize a few of the major marital adjustments that seem to me, after a generation of marriage counselling, to be of central importance. If you want to explore this kind of thing further, there are plenty of good books to read, and I have prepared for you a selected list with some guidance about what they contain.

As we try to understand what married life is all about, why

not start with sex? After all, without it, there would be no marriage at all.

Our New Understanding of Sex

A generation ago, the main purpose of marriage preparation was to make sure that the engaged couple knew the 'facts of life'. The ignorance in which young people were allowed to grow up in those days seems incredible as we look back on it. Girls really went into marriage with only the vaguest idea of where babies came from. Young men, especially those from strict religious homes, were sometimes almost completely ignorant about female anatomy and physiology, and had to find out how to function sexually by a process, often painful, of trial and error. To the less sensitive young man, marriage meant the opportunity to satisfy his sexual desires without restraint, and his young wife was expected to tolerate submissively whatever he did. The idea that the husband had a duty to make the experience pleasurable for his wife never entered his head. Few people had ever heard of the wife's sexual orgasm. I can recall counselling with a doctor who, when I explained to him that a woman could reach a climax in sexual intercourse very similar to that of her husband, was completely astounded. He had never imagined such a thing.

As knowledge about sexual functioning began to spread, the 'marriage manuals' began to be published. These books described the sex organs, internal and external, in detail and then went on to explain what happened in sexual intercourse. It became the fashion for couples about to marry to be given one of these books by their doctor or minister. Great emphasis was placed upon sexual technique, which explained to the husband-to-be, step by step, how to arouse his wife so that she could share his enjoyment of their sex relationship. The books were quite helpful, especially to those who would otherwise have entered marriage in almost complete ignorance. But what they had to say was, for too many couples, too little and too late. Those of us who were pioneers in marriage counselling in those early days knew only too well how many marriages were in trouble on account of all kinds of sexual difficulties. A doctor who worked with me for many years in London, and specialized in the treatment of sexual disharmony, estimated that as many as ninety per cent of all wives were unable to achieve orgasm. He proved to be quite wrong about this. But from the point of view of his practice, the steady stream of unhappy wives who sought his help seemed to justify his gloomy estimate.

Much has happened since those days, and we have made great progress in our understanding of sexual functioning. We tend to think of the sexual revolution in terms of an increase in pre-marital sex, and that is certainly true. But the really revolutionary thing that has happened has been the new understanding of sex that has come to married people. There can be no doubt that a remarkable transformation has taken place in their freedom to enjoy the physical expression of their love.

You who marry today may consider yourselves fortunate to be living in an era of enlightenment about this important aspect of marriage. The information that was so hard to get a generation ago is now common knowledge. In this book on marriage preparation, it seems unnecessary to devote more than one chapter to sex.

However, we had better not be too enthusiastic about the changes that have taken place, because our troubles are not entirely over. Married couples still come to me with sexual difficulties, mainly premature ejaculation and impotence in men, orgasm inadequacy in women. Masters and Johnson, whose recent researches have revolutionized our ideas about some areas of sexual functioning, suggest in their book on *Human Sexual Inadequacy* that as many as half of all married couples may still experience some trouble in achieving sexual adjustment, although they add more hopefully that sexual inadequacy could be almost eliminated in the next ten years.

Preparing for Marital Sex

What you are concerned about as a couple moving into marriage is what you can do now to ensure that this important part of your relationship will be satisfying to you both. Here are five areas for you to consider separately, and then discuss together in a joint session:

1. *Consider your own sex education to make sure it is adequate.* Sex education in the schools has been a long time coming, and it has suffered some setbacks when it did begin to be developed. It is probably certain, therefore, that you had no formal teaching on the subject that could be called anything like adequate. You have had to do your own private study of the subject, prompted by natural curiosity.

Now is the time to examine your knowledge, because this is a subject of primary importance for married people. Sex education normally covers four fields. You should have a reasonably clear understanding of the process of human reproduction and of the various methods of contraception. You should know the basic facts about the structure of the male and female sex organs and about sexual functioning. You should have enough knowledge about sex ethics to have established for yourself an acceptable code of personal behaviour. Finally, you should have some comprehension of the basic psychology of masculine and feminine attitudes and responses. These can all become vast subjects if studied in detail, and this is not at all necessary. But an elementary knowledge of all these areas is essential equipment for married life. Books covering this material are included in the list provided for your guidance.

2. *Make sure that your own individual attitudes to sex are*

sound and healthy. You have already made an evaluation of your past sexual experiences and how they have affected you. What is important now is to clear up any negative associations with sex which produce anxiety or guilt. You should feel comfortable and positive about your sexual nature and about the feelings and desires it stirs within you. There should be nothing here to be ashamed of or afraid of. If there is, it would be great wisdom for you to seek professional help about it. You owe it to your partner not to go into marriage unhappy, disturbed, or anxious about sex.

3. *Establish open communication between you about sexual feelings and responses.* Advice of this kind would not have been considered proper a generation ago. Today I offer it without hesitation. Two people going into marriage ought to be able to talk to each other quite freely, without embarrassment, about the way they affect each other sexually. Awkwardness and concealment here create confusion and misunderstanding. You two people have decided to bestow your sexuality upon each other, to be shared fully and without reserve for the rest of your lives. This is not something to be evasive about.

Talking together about this may, in fact, help you both a great deal in coming to terms with your own individual sexuality. The atmosphere of loving confidence and acceptance that should exist between you can do much to take away sexual anxiety and guilt.

4. *Insist upon reaching full agreement about whatever sexual experiences you're having together now.* I simply assume that you are having sexual experiences of some sort, though not necessarily full sexual intercourse. I would certainly support any couple who decide that waiting for marriage is the best plan for them. However, if we leave sexual intercourse on one side for a moment and consider other sexual intimacies short of intercourse, practically all couples looking toward marriages are having such experiences.

Exactly what you are doing together sexually is your own affair. All I am concerned about is what it may be doing to you. If you are both entirely happy about what is going on, free from any disquieting feelings, and blissfully contented with the pleasure you are giving each other, I have nothing more to say — unless you are taking risks that may lead to an undesired pregnancy. If, for example, you are having intercourse and not using a reliable contraceptive, you are taking chances, and in my opinion, acting irresponsibly. I don't happen to believe that a loving couple should conspire together to act irresponsibly, because this is very poor preparation for marriage.

Another thing I am concerned about is to make sure that one of you isn't in any way exploiting the other. This can easily happen, and it can be deeply damaging to your relationship. The usual situation is where he persuades her — against her better judgement — to have intercourse, though she would rather not do so. This is an unloving act, and it is made all the more hypocritical when he suggests to her that she is proving her love for him by letting him have his way. A woman treated in this fashion can easily develop a smouldering resentment that breaks down her confidence and trust in the man she loves. Anything of this kind — any taking advantage of each other to gain your sexual ends — is a dangerous misuse of sex that could spoil it for both of you in the end.

Sex is sheer enjoyment when fully shared by a loving couple. But it can become a destructive force in their relationship when one partner allows personal need to get out of control and imposes his or her will on the other. Handling sexual responses sensitively and sympathetically is not easy, but it is essential to a good sex life in marriage. If the management of sex before marriage sometimes puts self-control to a severe test, meeting that test successfully will strengthen your confidence. It will prove to you that you will be able, equally well, to cope with other situations that may arise in which, for love's sake, you have to forego having your own way. The capacity to consider the needs and wishes of the other as much as your own is of all qualities the one that matters most in marriage.

5. *Put the emphasis always on sex as experience and not as performance.* Our new knowledge of patterns of sexual response, while valuable in itself, has had one disturbing result. People are in danger of becoming upset if they fail to measure up to certain standards of performance and of judging each other in terms of whether or not they measure up. For many this has taken most of the joy and spontaneity out of sex and turned it into work rather than play. What is particularly distressing about this is that, when we turn sex into work and effort, it may respond by refusing to co-operate. At the root of nearly all the so-called psychosexual difficulties is the association of anxiety with sexual performance.

Each couple's sex life is something uniquely personal to them alone. Calculating frequencies of intercourse and counting orgasms may be appropriate for researchers, but for married couples it can have devastating results. I could tell harrowing stories of grimly anxious husbands consumed with anxiety because their wives didn't have what some books had said was the correct number of orgasms, and of outraged wives who complained that their husbands wanted to experiment with some daring departure from what has been called 'the missionary position'. One very wise and experienced doctor gave a clear answer on this latter point. 'Whatever is physiologically sound,' he declared, 'is also ethically right.' In other words, as long as you break no bones, it's OK.

Sex is the supreme expression of married love, and a loving couple are bound by no rules except their own sense of what brings them mutual happiness. If they are unable to agree about this, they need help.

Take time to talk over together the points I have raised in this chapter. If you can reach full agreement about this area of your relationship, this will prove to be a highly rewarding achievement.

9 How to Treat Your In-Laws

Someone once suggested a simple answer to this problem. 'Outlaw the in-laws,' he declared. Many of us would have to confess that there have been times when we have wished that we could do just that. But it wouldn't solve anything.

We have already discussed how you are each a product of your family background. The influence of your parents is not something you can cast off. It is part of you, built into your personality at deep, unconscious levels. So even if you rebel against them, even if you repudiate them, and treat them as strangers, they are still there, influencing your judgements and controlling your behaviour. Any psychotherapist can confirm this for you. It is a fact established on the basis of mountains of evidence. You had better accept it.

In-Law Problems Can Be Complicated

The implications of this for married couples are profound and far-reaching. There are no serious problems when both of you enjoy excellent relationships with your respective parents, your parents accept your marriage partner wholeheartedly, and the two sets of parents get along famously together. In these happy circumstances, there is agreement all round, and the in-laws lend their support to the married couple and give them a deep sense of security. This is the ideal arrangement, and it is not rare or exceptional. Many families have this sense of solidarity.

When Dr Evelyn Duvall made her study of in-law problems, she found that twenty-five per cent of all the married couples she approached reported that they could make no useful contribution to the study because their relationships with their in-laws were excellent and they had no problems at all.

However, problems often do arise. The ideal situation I have described is obviously the result of a fortunate combination of circumstances. Often enough this doesn't happen. There is a great deal that can go wrong. So let's look at the other side of the picture.

Sometimes everything goes wrong. Supposing both of you are in a state of strained relations with your parents, and the two sets of parents are not on speaking terms with each other. That would represent a situation full of conflict. Such situations are not rare or exceptional either. But apart from this extreme state of alienation all round, there can exist all sorts of intermediate groupings and alliances. If both of you are alienated from your parents, the parents on both sides may find a common bond in having rebellious children, and join forces in an effort to bring you both to reason. Then it becomes a straight conflict between the generations. Or the parents on one side may sympathize with you both about the hard treatment the parents on the other side are handing out. It is not even unusual to find one marriage partner supported by the parents of the other, who reject the behaviour of their own son or daughter.

Further complications can arise when the parents on one side, or even on both sides, are divided among themselves. Sometimes a mother will support her son while the father takes the side of his daughter-in-law. Or it may happen the other way round.

I have surely said enough to make it clear that this can be a very prickly problem area. And the solution isn't to cut yourself off from the in-laws. Parents can be a powerful stabilizing force in a marriage, and it is worth making great efforts to gain their acceptance and support. Patience and perseverance in this task may pay off handsomely in the end.

Every couple who have in-law problems should develop a strategy for dealing with them. The shadow of future conflict, if not the conflict itself, usually appears unmistakably on the horizon during the pre-marriage period. Sometimes this even proves to be the worst time of all, and the situation gets better after marriage. Sometimes the reverse is true.

A sound strategy must meet three basic requirements. First, it must be fully agreed upon and loyally acted upon by both of you. If one defaults, the strategy collapses and doesn't work. So your planning should be very thorough.

The second requirement is that the plan should be positive with the objective of achieving reconciliation and harmony, not retaliatory or punitive based on your angry and hurt feelings. The aim is not to reject the in-laws and shut them out of your lives, but if at all possible to win them over and create an atmosphere of mutual confidence and trust.

The third requirement is that your strategy should take account of the realities of the situation. These you should study carefully together. No two in-law problems are exactly alike. Yet there are frequently recurring factors that are common to most of them.

The Core of the Problem

Let me list the main facts about in-law tensions for your guidance in working out your own plan of campaign:

1. The person who causes most of these conflicts is unfortunately the mother-in-law. One study found that she initiated as much trouble as all the other in-laws put together. Fathers-in-law usually stay in the background, though sometimes they come helpfully to the rescue.

2. The victims of in-law interference are nearly always the daughters-in-law. It was from them, in the study I have mentioned, that nine out of ten of the complaints came. What most often happens is that the mother-in-law is jealous of her daughter-in-law for dividing the affection of her son, and tries to win back her central position in his life by alienating him from his wife. Unfortunately he sometimes finds it flattering to be the object of competition, and fails to take a firm stand against his mother's interference.

3. The competition and conflict between these two women reaches its most violent form when they have to live together in the same home. Doubling up with in-laws, if there is any likelihood of conflict, should therefore be firmly avoided. It just places too much strain on everyone concerned.

4. Another area in which the mother-in-law frequently interferes is in the rearing of the children. She does this by questioning their mother's child-rearing policies, or tries to buy the affection of the children by indulging them with gifts and special privileges.

5. The mother-in-law who acts in these ways can be very troublesome. But you should never lose sight of the fact that she is almost certainly deserving of your pity more than of your hostility. Again and again she turns out to be a very unhappy person. The typical example is a woman who never managed to develop a really close and mutually supportive relationship with her husband, and sought emotional fulfilment instead in caring for her children. Now that they are leaving her, she tries desperately to regain their attention and to get them back into her power. At the same time she is aware that she is beginning to grow old, and she may also be going

through the emotional upheavals of the menopause. She sees little to look forward to in her future, and therefore embarks on a campaign to achieve a sense of personal worth by gaining power over others. Most of this is done unconsciously -- she is not aware of her own motivations. What she really needs is the love of those around her, but since she seems unable to get it she tries instead to gain her ends by manipulation and intrigue. Unfortunately she usually doesn't realize that she is completely defeating her own purpose.

A Strategy for Avoiding Needless Conflict

Let me add now some working principles that have helped other couples to meet their in-law problems.

1. No in-law interference can damage a sound marriage. When husband and wife have an agreed policy and stand firmly together in putting it into effect, in-law attempts at exploitation and manipulation invariably fail. But any weakness, any crack in the unity of husband and wife, enables the in-laws to drive a wedge between them.

2. The policy to adopt is to make it clear that you want to be friendly and to work for harmony between the generations, but that you simply will not tolerate unwarranted interference in your marriage. This must be made unmistakably clear and no compromise tolerated. Sometimes this can only be done in a painful, out-in-the-open, once-and-for-all confrontation. When the in-laws have thus been shown decisively that their interference will not be tolerated, they usually give up and accept the situation.

3. This decisive confrontation should be followed up by sincere and genuine attempts to be friendly and conciliatory. Even if you simply don't like your in-laws as persons (and that isn't your fault), you can act in a kindly way towards them. We can all manage to be pleasant to people who are not congenial to us when we have to meet them socially or do business with them. Surely we can do at least as much in the cause of family unity. Many people make the mistake of thinking that if you have little in common with your in-laws, there is nothing you can do about it. In fact, you can behave lovingly even if you don't feel loving, and the action tends to promote the feeling. It will help and encourage your partner if you make a real and successful effort in this direction. Experience shows that this policy can in time achieve a surprising degree of success.

4. If you and your in-laws really have very little in common, the best way to maintain good relationships is to visit them from time to time, but always keep the visits brief. A congenial atmosphere can usually be maintained for a reasonably short period of time, particularly if you are all involved in doing something interesting together. But if you stay together too long with nothing to do, tensions may arise and goodwill may deteriorate rapidly.

5. Always remember that family ties cannot be broken, and last throughout a lifetime. Even if your relationships with your in-laws are not very congenial just now, a time may come when you may need their help or they may need yours. In the significant events of life, family members usually come together and participate; and in the crises of life, it is to them that we have the natural right to turn. You cannot predict what the future will

bring. The bonds that seem unimportant now may one day become a lifeline to you or to your children. It is wisdom to bend over backwards if necessary in order to keep the family relationships in good repair.

10 How to Manage Your Money

In the poorer cultures money represents the means of survival. But in our culture, where many people have more than they need in order to survive, it has also become an important status symbol. You measure your self-worth in terms of the amount and quality of the goods you are able to buy. Each of you already has developed a certain concept of what kind of expenditure is appropriate to your worth as a person. You know the kind of house and the kind of neighbourhood that would be right for you to live in, the kind of car you would like to own, the kind of clothes you want to wear. When your expenditure goes above what you consider to be appropriate, it makes you feel important, although at the same time you may also feel insecure. When your expenditure has to be on a lower scale than you feel you are entitled to, your self-esteem is wounded, and you feel outraged and insulted.

Two people may bring to marriage quite different money standards, and this can cause plenty of trouble. As long as you are spending your own money, what you do with it is your business. But if you and I are going into partnership, strains can soon develop. If I feel that you are buying something we can't afford, I'm going to protest. On the other hand, if you deny me the right to buy what I think I am entitled to, I am going to protest even more vigorously. Obviously, there is ample scope for disagreements here, and they are apt to be bitter disagreements, because they touch us in a very sensitive area –

that of our self-esteem.

The use of money, therefore, puts the partnership of marriage to one of its severest tests. So, unless you are in the fortunate position of having almost unlimited financial resources (and even then, your spending habits will tend to creep up till they reach the ceiling), you simply have to have an agreed policy. What money management really does is to test a couple's capacity to organize their joint life in a rational and orderly fashion – and surprising as it may seem, this is something most of us find peculiarly difficult.

Some Guidelines for a Financial Policy

I therefore suggest that, as part of your preparation for marriage, you work out together a plan that expresses your areas of agreement about financial policies, and I urge you particularly to look into any questions about which you are unable to reach agreement. To help you to get started, let me offer some suggestions that others have found helpful and that you might want to consider. Here is an outline of the issues in family finances on which you will have to make decisions if you are to have a workable policy.

1. *Do you favour sharing your income?* Some married couples keep their own money separately, and do not hold each other accountable for the way in which they spend it. The old-fashioned husband, quite often, didn't even tell his wife how much he earned. He doled out her weekly 'housekeeping money', and kept the rest of his pay. She had to meet all personal expenses out of 'housekeeping' or persuade her husband to give her any additional items she needed. Sometimes this was so humiliating that she built up a secret nest egg to give herself a sense of independence.

Modern couples share their income. This means you should both know all about the assets you jointly hold and the debts

91

you jointly owe. Without this basis of shared knowledge you can't even begin to formulate a joint policy.

You should discuss how far you can both accept the principle that all your assets really belong to both of you and also accept all debts as a joint responsibility. Are you both ready to assume, and to let the other assume, equal responsibility for all financial decisions? If not, why not?

2. *Who will be the treasurer?* You will need to have a policy for the actual handling of financial transactions. Traditionally the husband always paid the bills. But nowadays the wife often does this, and the husband may be glad to be relieved of the responsibility. Some couples decide who will manage the money on the basis of who is best equipped for this task, regardless of sex. It is possible also, of course, for both to pay bills out of separate accounts or by writing cheques on a joint account. If this policy is adopted, it is as well to have a clear understanding about the areas in which each is entitled to make payments. Otherwise confusion may well arise. A bill may go unpaid because each thought the other dealt with it, or a bill may even be paid twice over.

3. *What will your budget look like?* Working out a hypothetical budget is such a good way of discovering each other's basic attitudes to money management that I seriously suggest that you spend an evening or two together on it. I believe you would learn a great deal about each other in the process.

Begin by estimating as nearly as you can what your joint income might add up to. Then make estimates as accurately as you can of all the basic expenditure that would have to come out of this income: housing, light and heat, furnishings, food, clothes, personal items, car, holidays, insurance, savings, and the like. Then see how income and expenditure are likely to balance out and how effectively you could manage to live within your income.

This cannot be done precisely, of course. So the exercise

should not be taken too seriously. The aim is to find out how far you can reach agreement and where your areas of conflict in money management are likely to be. A good idea, when a group of couples is involved, is for each couple to work separately on their budget and then for all to meet for a general discussion of the principles and methods of money management.

4. *What about personal allowances?* One of the most perplexing questions in the area of family finance is how to deal with small personal items such as haircuts, drinks, cigarettes, hobbies, gifts, entertainment, and such. To put so many small items into a budget is tedious and time-consuming. They are hard to estimate in advance, and most of us thoroughly dislike having to make an entry in a notebook every time we buy a postage stamp or put a coin in a parking meter.

The best solution to this problem seems to be to give each member of the family (including children when they are old enough) a personal allowance, weekly or monthly, which they can use for these small items, and for which they don't have to keep records. Finding out how much represents a fair allowance can be done only by experiment, and you have to be flexible about this until you get it right. The system, however, seems to work better than any other. If the wife doesn't earn any of the family income, it is good for her to have an allowance that she can really call her own. And having a regular weekly allowance helps children at an early age to learn the value of money, and how to manage it wisely.

It is necessary to decide just what range of items is to be bought out of these personal allowances. This usually includes recreation. Some families make it big enough to include clothes as well. Other families budget separately for clothes, and at least for recreation in which all share together.

5. *What is your attitude toward debt?* In the time of our grandparents the custom was to pay cash down, and it was

considered disgraceful to get into debt, except for such major items as a mortgage on the family home. Now all that has changed, and many people buy most major items – furniture, cars, appliances, and the like – on the basis of payment with interest extended over a period of time. It has become quite respectable to buy now and pay later.

There is another side to this. Families on marginal incomes often get into serious trouble by using this system. Married couples have endless quarrels about how to meet the mounting total of monthly payments and to buy food to eat as well. Often the amount of interest paid out consumes a sizeable proportion of a man's weekly earnings. And when the facts are realistically faced, many of the goods purchased were not really needed at all.

Most married couples have to decide firmly, sooner or later, where to take a stand on this question of debt. It could prevent a lot of later misery if you could agree on a sound policy now.

6. *What are your insurance needs?* Insurance makes good sense, and brings peace of mind. But we need so much of it these days that the overcautious can easily find themselves 'insurance poor'. There are life insurance, home insurance, car insurance, and many others. Where do you stop?

Insurance needs have to be seen in proportion, in relation to each other, and in relation to available income. There are flexible plans available for almost every possible situation, but you have to know about them and understand them, or you can make foolish mistakes.

7. *Do you plan to buy a home?* Housing costs have soared to alarming heights these days, and many young couples feel that home ownership is right out of their reach. Yet having a place you can call your own brings to a family one of its deepest and most lasting satisfactions. Buying a home is also a good way of building up savings, because if it is a good house in a good neighbourhood, its value should go up steadily, and it would be

a saleable item in a dire emergency. On the other hand, if the breadwinner's job calls for the possibility of a number of moves, renting a flat could be a better plan. You should weigh these issues carefully in the light of your personal prospects.

In the old days, married couples were usually content to start housekeeping with a few inexpensive items of furniture and equipment and to replace these later when there was a little more money in the bank. Nowadays, many newly married couples feel that they must have a houseful of brand new, high quality equipment from the start, and in order to achieve this they put themselves under a crippling burden of debt. You should consider seriously what policy makes sense for you.

8. *What about savings?* The average married couple, in addition to meeting their day-to-day expenses, need during their lifetime to plan savings for three major purposes. First, they should aim at owning a home of their cwn someday. Second, they may need the means to give their children a good start in life. Third, they will need resources for their retirement years. It is as well to face these contingencies from the very beginning, and to have a sound plan to meet them. I know that most of us are helped in these days by compulsory forms of saving like Social Security and pension plans. But these usually provide only a basic amount, and may need to be supplemented if we want to enjoy anything like the standard of living to which we have grown accustomed.

A savings policy means an investment policy, and here we are in a very complex field in which I cannot claim to be qualified to guide you. What you need here is the advice of a well-informed person who is not going to sell you anything – the man with something to sell will naturally wish to direct your thoughts toward the merits of his product. Be cautious, too, about accepting the advice of your personal friends or colleagues whose knowledge of investing may be no more reliable than their own limited experience.

Summary

Happy indeed are those who never had a disagreement about money. The best way to join their ranks is to discuss the whole question thoroughly now and to reach if possible an agreed policy on the various aspects of the subject which I have raised with you.

Remember, however, that money itself is not the trouble. Money is simply a useful device to facilitate the exchange of goods and services. Your quarrels and disagreements on financial matters are always the reflection of conflict in your relationship. Don't, therefore, be satisfied with solutions in terms of money policy alone. Try always to get behind the money itself to the reasons why you are using it as a battleground. Clear up the underlying conflicts, and with a basic amount of sound knowledge and good judgement you will be able to handle your financial affairs satisfactorily.

11 A Few More Problem Areas

A wise old social worker once said to me, 'Marriage problems? I've been dealing with them all my life. If you ask me, they all boil down to three problem areas: sex, in-laws, and money.'

These are the problem areas we have discussed so far, and they certainly are the ones about which most married people seem to need help. But there are plenty of other problem areas. I don't see any need to give you a long list of them, because you are not exactly looking for trouble. However, there are a few that you ought to know about, and I will draw your attention to them, quite briefly, in this chapter.

Children

The blessing of parenthood has always been highly prized, and having children is normally a great joy to a husband and wife. Yet this area of married life can cause trouble too.

Few people ever try to analyse their reasons for wanting children. If they did, they would find quite a variety of motives. The wish to perpetuate your identity, keeping up with the neighbours, proving your manhood or womanhood, providing someone to care for you in your old age – these are some of the motives which we don't generally acknowledge. You might like to talk this over together. Do you both really want children? What are your main reasons? Are you substantially in agree-

4

ment about this? You had better be. Unresolved conflict in this area can be very painful.

How many children would you like to have? The days of the big family seem to be about over. Studies suggest that three children is the number most often wanted nowadays. But since the population problem has been brought so prominently to our attention, some people are campaigning for no more than two children to each couple. What is your view about this?

Then there is the matter of spacing the children in a family. I assume you will get some sound advice from your doctor about birth control, and I need not discuss this in detail. But you still must make some decisions. Will you try to start a family right away after marriage? Or do you follow the school of thought that advocates waiting a year or so, either to make your early marital adjustments without the complications of pregnancy, or so that the wife can accumulate a small capital reserve from her earnings. There are good arguments on both sides, and I wouldn't want to influence you either way.

What if you should want children, but none come? Then you should ask your doctor for a full investigation of your fertility. Both of you should be tested. These days, it is usually possible to locate the trouble, and in many cases it can be cleared up. Failing that, you have to choose between an adoption, artificial insemination if it is the husband who is sterile, or a childless marriage. The latter choice needn't be a tragedy. It may surprise you to know that, according to some studies, childless marriages prove to be a shade happier than those with children.

Conflicts over bringing up the children arise in many marriages. But we counsellors find that this is usually a projection of conflicts already present between the couple. The coming of children, according to the findings of many researchers, intensifies the existing state of the marriage. If the couple are happy together, children tend to increase that happiness. If the marriage is unhappy, children unfortunately are likely to make it more so.

Work

Married people labour in two fields, in the home and outside it. The traditional pattern was that the wife was responsible for the housework, while the husband went out and earned the money.

That pattern has changed a good deal. In fact, there is no clear pattern any more. So you will have to work out your own. If the wife is going to be what we call gainfully employed, will the husband help out at the homemaking end? Some men don't like domestic duties. Yet the wife naturally feels let down if she works in both spheres, and her husband works in only one.

Another factor is that some men feel it to be a reflection on their masculinity if they don't support their wives, and they resent the wife wanting to take an outside job. Yet the wife often needs the job not just to earn money but also to feel that she is doing something significant in the world, and perhaps putting her education and training to good use. If she stays at home, she may suffer from what Margaret Mead has called the 'trapped housewife syndrome'.

Then there is the question of whether a mother who goes out to work is neglecting her children. It was once thought that children suffered severely when the mother was absent for part of the day. Now we know that with really adequate day-care and wise use of the time when the mother is at home, the children need not suffer at all. Some argue that they will actually be better off because a mother who goes out into the world will be better equipped to guide her children as they go out into the world.

There are pros and cons on all these questions. If the issue is one that is likely to concern you, it would be wise to discuss it thoroughly before marriage and reach agreement about the policy you favour.

Friends

During this period you naturally want to spend a lot of time by yourselves. But once married, the question of your social life has to be decided. Many a man takes the view that once he has won his fair lady and settled her in a home, he can return to his old cronies and spend most of his spare time with them. But the wife may not see it in this light, so there is trouble. If he persists, she may establish her own separate social life, and before long they are drifting apart.

While former associates need not be dropped, it helps a marriage if husband and wife can build new friendships on a couple basis. When people get married they cross a sort of invisible line. The focus of their life changes, they develop new interests, and it becomes inappropriate to go back to the old carefree bachelor patterns. If both can make the transition smoothly together, all will be well. But if one is ready to make it and the other isn't, there can be trouble.

Then there's the knotty question of friends of the opposite sex. Jealousy can cause havoc between married couples, and you need to have a clear understanding about how you both regard such friendships in any depth. In these swinging days of mate-swapping, some couples seem to be very permissive about such matters. It is dangerous, however, to assume that any but a small minority of people take this point of view.

Married couples certainly need to have their circle of friends. 'Two people wrapped up in each other,' someone has said, 'make a very small parcel.' But the choice of these friends, the activities shared with them, and the time devoted to them –

these questions need to be settled with the full agreement of both of you.

Recreation

One aspect of the question of outside friends is the use of leisure time. Some couples have common interests and like to spend their evenings together pursuing their hobbies. Usually this is good for their marriage. It avoids the danger that otherwise all their time together might have to be devoted to household chores, making routine decisions, and coping with family problems.

However, when the leisure interests of husband and wife take them in opposite directions, what then? To a reasonable extent, by common agreement, they can live with this. If they can get each other interested in their respective pursuits, they can at least report on their significant experiences afterwards without boring each other. But sometimes the point comes at which individual sacrifices must be made for the sake of the marriage. I remember my own personal predicament in a situation of this kind when I found soon after marriage that my wife was feeling lonely and neglected on Saturday afternoons when I left her to play football. This disturbed me, and I finally dropped out of the team. Instead we started going for long country hikes together on Saturday afternoons, which we both enjoyed very much.

The question of holidays comes up here, also. Some people like to seek the gay life of the city, others prefer the solitude of the mountains. Some love to travel abroad, some feel more secure at home. Some love camping, some hate it. When two people marry with radically different preferences, what do they do? I think an occasional separate holiday is a reasonable compromise, but to make a habit of it may lead to complications.

Leisure hours are coming these days to add up to a lot of total time. Planning to use it wisely may be an important contribution to the success of your marriage.

Personal Habits

We are always being told the story of the marriage that broke up because the husband insisted that the bedroom window should be open all night and the wife was equally determined to keep it closed. It isn't really true that such differences can break a marriage. It is the immovable stubbornness in both that makes it impossible for them to live together. And if they slept in a bedroom with no windows at all, they would still find something else to fight about.

If minor irritants of this kind don't break marriages, however, they certainly can wear down goodwill and cool affection. An otherwise loving wife who disapproves of alcohol is going to be anything but loving when her husband comes home drunk. A husband who thinks smoking is unpleasant and an unhealthy habit isn't going to be motivated to kiss his wife when she reeks of tobacco. The man who has to catch the 7:10 to the office each morning is going to get annoyed if his wife keeps him up talking till midnight, and the compulsively tidy housewife will be exasperated by the husband who leaves his discarded clothes lying all over the bedroom and bathroom floor.

Some annoying personal habits usually show up before marriage, and that's a good time to face them squarely. Otherwise the annoyance will certainly be intensified in the closer and more continuous shared life of marriage. Most of your personal habits are not ingrained, and you should be willing to change them, or at least modify them, to please the one you love most. Unwillingness to accommodate yourself in these matters may be interpreted as meaning that you don't care; and if you don't care, the next question is how much do you really love? People

102

who expect to go into marriage without making any changes in their living patterns just don't understand what marriage is all about. If we say we love each other, the best proof of it is our willingness to try hard to be pleasing in the way we behave.

Summary

I have given you some examples of the adjustments to each other that married people have to be willing to make in order to live happily and harmoniously together. You don't need to take all of them too seriously because many may never arise in your particular case, but you will have adjustments to make and some of them will be irksome. This fact you had better understand clearly.

There are two good reasons why you should spend some time now, before you marry, in trying to identify some of your potential problem areas. The first is that by knowing in advance what the task of marriage is likely to involve, you will be spared the shattering sense of 'let down' you might otherwise suffer when these discouraging realities can no longer be evaded. By preparing for them in advance, you will be equipped with well-formulated policies to deal with them when the time comes.

The other reason for facing these issues now is that you really don't have to wait till marriage to make all of these adjustments to each other. Some adjustment problems, I am sure, have already come up between you. Many couples adopt the philosophy of 'have fun now, work later' and shelve the problems. You should consider whether this really is a good approach. If you do some of the work now, you can still have fun; and you will very much ease the later task of marital adjustment by doing some of your homework in advance.

12 Some Parting Words

Well, that's it! I have now gone over with you both the questions I would have raised with you if you had actually come to me together for marriage preparation, and we had set up a series of interviews. I have not, of course, gone into medical questions that concern your doctor nor into religious questions which your minister will discuss with you. But I have tried to give you basic marriage preparation which can be supplemented, according to your need, by reading to gain further information and by face-to-face counselling in some particular area.

I've set you a lot of homework to do, separately and together. Just by way of a final reminder, let me list the assignments I have suggested to you:

1. *Your Individual Marriageability.* To determine this, I asked each of you to make an individual self-evaluation covering nine areas which we went over in chapter 5. I asked you to do this separately in writing, then to meet, and – as far as you felt you could – to share your notes with each other.

2. *Your Compatibility as a Couple.* In chapter 6 I asked you to consider, separately and then together, the following areas: your personal experiences with the mate selection process, what you do and do not have in

common, and your emotional complementarity.

3. *Your Marital Expectations.* In chapter 7 I suggested you should – again separately and then together – look at your goals and plans for your marriage; first, sharing lists of your individual expectations, then discussing what type of marriage, in terms of involvement, you both want; and finally using areas of disagreement to put in some practice in the all-important art of conflict resolution.

4. *Your Marital Adjustments.* Finally, I set you the task of looking ahead and trying to decide how you would handle together a whole series of adjustments you will have to make if your marriage is to succeed, and most of which you can begin working on now. Specifically, I gave you the following items for discussion: your sexual attitudes (chapter 8), your in-law strategy (chapter 9), your financial policy (chapter 10), your approach to parenthood, your division of labour, and your attitudes towards friends, recreation, and personal habits which you may find irritating in one another (chapter 11). This is not meant to be an exhaustive list. You could add many other important questions, such as religious practices and political loyalties. However, I do not personally consider these tasks of marriage to be as important as your personal feelings and attitudes to each other, so I have put them last. In the past, the tendency has been to put too much stress on these practical matters. My view is that, if once you can really get your inner selves in tune with each other, you should be able to cope together with most situations you are confronted with. Whereas you will never cope with anything, but turn every situation into a battleground, if you have not achieved inner harmony with each other.

You will notice that I have made no attempt to give you anything like a scorecard. Many marriage books include some kind of quiz with points you can score on each question and then add up, comparing your total with something like a national average. This can be interesting and useful, but I can't feel personally very enthusiastic about it. I believe it is more helpful simply to confront you with the issues we know to be important for the making of a successful marriage, ask you to discuss them seriously together, and then leave you to draw your own conclusions. I have almost always found that, through this kind of process, people develop awareness of what are the promising and the threatening factors in their relationship. Indeed, almost invariably they were already instinctively aware of these things, but often had not examined their own feelings or looked at their possible implications. People who are very much in love live very intensely in the present and are not inclined to contemplate implications. But if they plan to marry, they simply must do so. High moments when you can go hand-in-hand singing into the moonlight are great. But such sweet and tender love can have no assured future unless it is anchored to the realities of every day living in a very complicated world. This is what getting ready for marriage means.

What Have You Learned?

Well, what do you now know about your state of readiness for marriage? After all those hours of self-examination and discussion, you will be an exceptional couple indeed if you have passed all the tests with flying colours. You would hardly be human if you had not turned up some areas in which you feel poorly prepared for marriage. The experiences of self-examination and mutual evaluation you have been through should have brought those areas clearly into the open, which was what they were intended to do.

You will now need to decide together what to do about any areas of your relationship that don't measure up to your expectations. You should try to determine whether these problem areas are caused by aspects of your individual lives or of your interaction with each other that can be changed so as to make the prospect more promising. If you think the necessary changes can be made, work out a plan that can put this to the test, now or later. In doing this, you will have to consider whether this is something you can achieve by yourselves or whether you should have professional help. In general, it is sound policy to deal with your problems yourselves so long as you find you can make acceptable progress. The effort provides you with a good learning experience and enables you to develop problem-solving techniques that may help you later in other situations.

However, if by your own unaided efforts you fail to make the progress you expect and hope for, you will reach a critical point at which it is essential to act. If at the point when your own resources have not proved adequate you do not seek help, you may soon be in serious trouble, with disillusionments turning you sour and causing a deterioration of your whole relationship. It is the height of folly to let this happen and not to seek the aid of a person with specialized knowledge. A skilled counsellor may be able relatively easily to see why you are failing and put you on the right track. There is no merit whatever in suffering needlessly just because you cannot bring yourself to ask for help.

Even if you have a few problems which you can't solve, either with or without help, you will not be an unusual couple. No marriage is perfect. Many divorced persons who later re-married have told me that the second marriage really was no better than the first, but by that time they had learned to be more tolerant, to scale down their expectations to reasonable proportions, and to make the best of what they had. Marriage partners are fallible human beings – often weak and sometimes wayward – and we have to bear and forbear. If your assets on the whole significantly exceed your liabilities and the liabilities are of such a nature that time should liquidate at least some of them, you probably have the raw materials out of which many couples have, with patience and perseverance, made good and happy marriages. As someone once put it, if you can't realize your ideal, idealize your real.

However, what if your evaluations leave you with the definite impression that you just don't have what it takes to achieve an acceptable marriage? Then you are faced with a very difficult situation. Since subjective judgements are not always reliable, you might want to test this out with a marriage counsellor. However, it is only fair to say that if you arrive at the conclusion that you just aren't right for each other, your judgement is probably correct, because such a judgement doesn't come easily and runs contrary to the normal hopes of the engaged couple who tend to take a very rosy view of the situation and minimize any negative factors.

If as your counsellor I have brought you to this unhappy state of mind, I offer no apologies. I hate to cause you pain and distress, but I am fully convinced that if this is your honest conclusion, it is far better to have reached it now than to have evaded it and had to face it after the marriage had taken place and possibly children had been born. It is far, far better to break a relationship than to embark on a doubtful marriage. If two people later come to the conclusion that they were right for each other after all, they can come together again with no serious harm done. In my experience, however, this is a rare event. Most people who break up tend later to be reinforced in their decision, rather than the contrary.

My expectation, however, is that most of the couples who take this book seriously and do their homework, will have the potential for a good marriage. My purpose in entering into this counselling relationship with you has been to help you to take the steps that will enable you to make the very most of your potential and develop the kind of close and warm relationship that will be deeply rewarding to you both. It is this kind of experience that would be my wish for you.

Communication and Loyalty

As we take leave of each other, what all-important message can I leave with you? I have often been asked what is the one thing, above all others, that can ensure a successful marriage? I have always found this an awkward question, because there are many ingredients that contribute to success in marriage, and what is all-important for any given couple depends on their particular set of circumstances.

I asked one of my fourth year medical students, who read the manuscript of this book and whose judgement I consider to be very sound, what I ought to stress most. His answer was that the most important issue in early marriage was communication, the need for the couple to be open and honest with each other and to keep the flow of feeling and thought moving freely between them. I have no quarrel with that judgement. As I have already pointed out, most marriages in trouble turn out to have failed primarily in this area, and the major function of marriage counselling, as I understand it, is to help the couple to clear the clogged channels and get the flow of feeling going again between them.

Yet I am not content to let that be my parting word to you. There is something else I want to stress that is perhaps more important to couples starting out in marriage. The word that best expresses it is loyalty.

I once wrote an article in which I said that loyalty is the acid test of a marriage, and I still think this is profoundly true. Marriage is, in the end, the coming together of two people in the quest for the deepest kind of human relationship that can be found – a full self-giving of each to the other and a uniting of two lives in the closest intimacy. Not all couples wish for this, or would tolerate this. But I am speaking of marriage at its best, and marriage at its best has a tremendous appeal because it has so much to offer.

In this quest, I see loyalty as the central quality. How can love and trust be sustained without loyalty? Loyalty is the dependable devotion you give to your closest friend, to the cause you esteem above all others. It is a pledge you make to yourself that you won't let the other person down, that you won't exploit that person or take a mean advantage. It is this kind of determination to stand by each other and to work at the marriage and make it succeed that is lacking too often today and that lies, in my opinion, behind a great many of the failures. There are marriages that simply won't work, and this sad fact has to be faced in the end. But to start out in marriage with one eye on the escape hatch is no way to succeed; for marriage, as I have surely made clear by this time, is a tough, difficult undertaking, a task that will yield success only to those who put their heart and soul into it.

Many years ago, I read a book on marriage by the famous French writer André Maurois, in which he summed this up rather neatly. He spoke of the years in which young people date each other and rate each other, and then, in the fullness of time, they make their choice of the one they want to marry. Now they have reached a turning point in life. If they know what they are doing and are serious about it, they will say, 'I have chosen; from now on my aim will be, not to search for someone who will please me, but to please the one I have chosen.'

If two people, having chosen each other and being satisfied

that their choice is a sound one, are quite determined to please each other – in the fullest and deepest sense of the word – it's rather difficult, isn't it, to imagine how they could fail?

Appendix I

People Who Can Help You

In this book I have tried to act as your pre-marital counsellor without ever seeing you or meeting you personally.

Only you can say how far this experience has been helpful. If you feel that it has provided you with the preparation for marriage you needed, and you have not become aware of any problems you can't handle by yourselves, I am satisfied. But if you now recognize that you need some further help, I want to continue to be your counsellor by showing you how you can find it. I can do this in two ways.

First, I have prepared for you a list of books to which you can turn for further reading. Through such reading you can become students of the most distinguished authorities. The list in Appendix 2 includes a few comments about each book, so that you may have some idea of where to turn for the particular information you need.

Marriage Guidance Councils

The other way of guiding you to further help is to refer you to an actual counsellor with whom you can work on some of the more knotty problems that may have come up. Fortunately in Britain we have local Marriage Guidance Councils in most communities, and there you will find the help you need.

Let me offer some general comments about other professional people, not necessarily specialists in marriage counselling, whose help you might seek.

Your Minister

In all matters relating to preparation for marriage, your minister is likely to be your best friend, and you would be wise to discuss with him anything you plan to do. Ministers conduct weddings, and they are well aware of the importance of adequate preparation for the adjustments of married life. There is little doubt that ministers, priests, and rabbis undertake far more marriage preparation than all members of the other professions combined.

Many ministers routinely invite the couple to meet with them before the wedding. Some have been thoroughly trained in pre-marital counselling and do an excellent job. Others, lacking training, do their best, but it isn't as thorough as they would wish. One of my hopes is that some ministers may find it helpful to use this book as a means of venturing further into the field than they have done before and of giving better service to their young people.

Your minister will, of course, go over the wedding service with you in advance and interpret to you just what it means. He will also probably set up a wedding rehearsal. By these means you will be set free from needless anxiety or uncertainty about how to act when the time comes. This should enable you to participate wholeheartedly in the ritual, making the wedding a happy and memorable occasion as it should be.

Apart from the wedding ceremony, your minister can be a good friend to you in the process of leaving your parental home and setting up your own new home. Churches in these days are becoming more and more family-centred in their emphasis. Don't hesitate to turn to your minister for any help you may need, now or later, as you venture forth into the state of matrimony.

Your Doctor

Doctors in general don't have the same close contact as ministers do with people about to marry. A number of questions arise, however, about which a doctor's help may be needed before marriage. Let me refer to some of these:

1. *General examination.* Some people think it is a good plan, before marriage, for both partners to have a complete physical check-up, and to 'exchange health certificates'. Marriage involves the sharing of life, and the reasoning is that if you are taking each other 'for better or worse', each of you should know the medical outlook for the other. This is obvious in cases where one partner has some disease or disability which reduces or hinders the capacity to live a normal life, but there may also be factors in a person's physical make up which, while not now interfering with normal functioning, could do so later. By putting all the cards on the table now, you can avoid any possible misunderstanding or recrimination later. This makes good sense.

2. *Genital examination.* Many women go to a gynaecologist for a check up prior to marriage. The doctor can quickly identify any condition of the sex organs that might need attention. If the woman is a virgin, she may possibly have a resistant hymen that will not stretch or break easily, and this could spoil the honeymoon by making penetration by the penis impossible. The doctor can deal with the trouble very simply, using only a local anaesthetic. Other malformations of the female sex organs (fortunately these are quite rare) can be recognized and dealt with.

The usual purpose of her visit to her doctor, however, is in order to get his advice about birth control. When the diaphragm was the most widely used method, a fitting was required. The pill at present has to be prescribed by a doctor, and the I.U.D. (intra-uterine device) put in place by him. So birth control is still, for most women, the primary service for which they turn to their doctors.

A genital examination is not normally required by the husband-to-be. Unless obvious abnormalities of the sex organ are present, the physician cannot make any reliable predictions about its capacity to function. Problems of male sex adjustment are in the great majority of cases emotional in origin.

3. *Sex techniques.* Both partners sometimes seek a consultation with their doctor in order to ensure that their sex education is adequate, and particularly to talk over sexual anxieties and uncertainties. All doctors are not equally well equipped to give this kind of help, but some who have specialized in the field can be the best possible counsellors and can give the couple help and reassurance that should be of great value to them. Those who are not inclined to do this kind of counselling themselves can usually refer the couple to someone who will do so.

4. *Genetic examination.* Occasionally a couple, sure that they want to marry each other, are not equally sure that they ought to have children, because in the family background of one or of both there is evidence of inherited disease or defect. Anxieties of this kind can be distressing, and it is a wise plan to get the expert opinion of a specialist in genetics. Considerable progress has been made in recent years in the understanding of these inherited conditions, and we are now able to make some fairly accurate predictions which can help a couple to estimate the percentage of risk that children born to them would suffer from inherited disability. Your doctor can refer you to a geneticist.

Other Professional Helpers

The basic members of the marriage preparation team are the marriage counsellor, the minister, and the doctor. You should not hesitate to seek their advice and co-operation. Getting married, as some of the wedding rituals remind us, is a highly responsible undertaking, not to be embarked upon lightly or irresponsibly. The success of your marriage is a matter far too important to leave to chance, and when there are people in your community whose assistance could make all the difference between success or failure, between happiness and misery, it is folly not to seek that help and to make use of it.

Additional helpers can be sought when special needs must be met. Personality problems are best handled by the clinical psychologist or the psychiatrist. Legal difficulties obviously lie in the sphere of the lawyer, and this is no place for do-it-yourself efforts. Financial tangles also call for expert guidance, and your bank should be able to put you in touch with someone who can provide this.

Modern social workers are often very versatile people and include in their ranks men and women with a wide variety of specialized skills. It is in fact surprising and reassuring to investigate the impressive array of services which modern communities provide to help people, covering almost every conceivable kind of human need. Few of these services existed a generation ago. Many of them still do not exist in other countries. You are fortunate to be living in a land so rich in resources. It is your privilege to make good use of them.

Appendix II

Books For Your Further Reading

The books and booklets listed below are normally available at the National Marriage Guidance Council's Book Department, Little Church Street, Rugby, which is open to callers between 9 a.m. and 5 p.m. Monday to Friday. It provides a reliable service for those wanting the best literature on marriage and the family. The books may also be obtained by post.

Belliveau, F., and Richter, L. *Understanding Human Sexual Inadequacy*. Hodder Books. 242 pages. Clear explanation of Masters and Johnson therapy, which is based on new techniques of understanding and helping sexual difficulties.

Berne, Eric. *Sex in Human Loving*. Penguin. 268 pages. Understanding and amusing explanation of how and why we fall into different patterns of sexual behaviour.

Bevan, James, MA, MB, BChir (Cantab), D(Obst), RCOG, MCGP. *Sex, the Plain Facts*. Faber. 96 pages. A clear and accurate factual description for young people in late teens or early twenties.

Chaloner, Len. *First Year of Life*. NMGC. 16 pages. How babies begin feeling and thinking.

Chartham, Robert. *Mainly for Women*. Sphere Book. 158 pages. Describes the woman's part in the sex relationship and how she can fulfil her responsibility for making it successful.

Chartham, Robert. *Sex Manners for Men.* New English Library. 144 pages. Outspoken guide to love making.

Chesser, Eustace, Dr. *Love Without Fear.* Arrow Books. 320 pages. A guide to sexual technique, reassurance about what is normal and a useful list of definitions of sexual terms.

Consumer Association. *Pregnancy Month by Month.* 106 pages.

Fletcher, Peter. *Emotional Problems.* Pan Books, 1972. 197 pages. Helpful guide to understanding personal problems and relief of nervous suffering.

Greengross, W., Dr. *Sex in Early Marriage.* NMGC. 36 pages.

Griffith, E. F., MRCS, LRCP. *Modern Marriage.* Methuen, 1972. 280 pages.

Harris, Thomas A. *I'm OK – You're OK.* Pan, 1969. 269 pages. In non-technical language how to control yourself, your relationships and your future. A guide to transactional analysis.

Kenner, Jill. *Goodbye to the Stork.* NMGC. 92 pages. An invaluable guide to parents about the sex education of their children. Jill Kenner writes for parents of children of all ages and shows how the subject can be tackled, questions answered and information given to four-year-olds as well as late teenagers.

Llewellyn-Jones, D. *Everywoman, A Gynaecological Guide for Life.* Faber. 316 pages. Well illustrated and covers the medical side of a woman's life but specially good on the period from puberty and marriage to childbirth.

Mace, David. *Sexual Difficulties in Marriage.* NMGC. 54 pages. New methods of helping couples solve their sexual problems.

Mace, David. *Whom God Hath Joined.* Epworth Press, 1973. 94 pages. A book of daily readings to be used by a husband and wife in early married life.

NMGC. *Sex in Marriage.* 58 pages. A comprehensive guide to sexual technique.

O'Neill, Nena and George. *Open Marriage*. Peter Owen, 1973. 287 pages. Personal freedom and a new life style in marriage.

Spicer, Faith. *Sex and the Love Relationship*. Priory Press. Sex in its true perspective within the love relationship as a whole.

Stone, Hannah and Abraham, Drs. *A Marriage Manual*. Gollancz. 307 pages. New edition of the famous handbook which is a practical guide to sex and marriage in question and answer form.

Toft, Mogens, and Fowlie, J. *Sexual Techniques*. Souvenir Press. 144 pages. A fully illustrated guide to love.

Tuffill, S. G. *Sexual Stimulation in Marriage*. Mayflower. 187 pages. Very frank book based on letters from Forum Magazine.

Wallis, J. H. *Thinking About Love*. Routledge. 168 pages. Cloth and paper. Understanding the rewards and difficulties of the emotional aspects of love.

Wallis, J. H. *Sexual Harmony in Marriage*. Routledge. 132 pages. Not about techniques but the deeper personal relationship between husband and wife.

Which *Guide to Contraceptives*. Third Revised Edition. 79 pages. Comprehensive guide to all methods of birth control.